FOL 5

To:

_____

From:

_____

Date:

_____

YOU'RE GOING *to* MAKE *it*

50 MORNING AND EVENING DEVOTIONS
TO UNRUSH YOUR MIND, UNCOMPLICATE YOUR HEART, AND EXPERIENCE HEALING TODAY

Lysa TerKeurst

THOMAS NELSON

Since 1798

Published in Nashville, Tennessee, by Thomas Nelson. Thomas Nelson is a registered trademark of HarperCollins Christian Publishing, Inc.

Photographs by Meshali Mitchell

Thomas Nelson titles may be purchased in bulk for educational, business, fund-raising, or sales promotional use. For information, please email SpecialMarkets@ThomasNelson.com.

ISBN 978-1-4002-3911-5 (audiobook)
ISBN 978-1-4002-3909-2 (eBook)
ISBN 978-1-4002-3908-5 (HC)

Printed in India
23 24 25 26 27 REP 12 11 10 9 8 7 6 5 4 3

This book is dedicated to one of my favorite places to go when my soul needs to breathe and my heart needs to heal.

To: Bald Head Island, North Carolina:

I wanted to capture where my life intersected with your breathtaking beauty that is so simple and yet so very vast. From the first moment I took the ferry into your harbor, you seemed to whisper to me, "Welcome home. You're going to make it." God's fingerprints are especially noticeable to me in all He created your island to be. And His presence is felt here by all who slow down enough to experience it.

You've helped me heal in the most tender and sacred parts of my heart. It's like you knew I needed to see that you've survived the fiercest of storms, too, and are still standing as beautiful as ever. That revelation helped me feel safe enough to laugh again, hope again, and find the joy of building both sandcastles and dreams again.

Every photograph in this book was taken on Bald Head Island and means something very special to me. If you ever get a chance to visit, and I hope you will, make sure to wave in my direction. And when in doubt, definitely order the key lime pie.

Contents

DAY **1**

Healing Is Not
as Neat and
Tidy as I'd Like

Your word is a lamp for my feet, a light on my path.

PSALM 119:105

MORNING

I love God's Word. And I do trust God.

I must tell you, though, some of the unknowns of my life right now make me tremble with raw nerves and shaky hands. My biggest unknowns are questions still unanswered. *Will I always carry the grief of what's been lost and taken during this last season of my life? How will I know when I'm healed, and how long will healing take?*

Healing is not nearly as neat and tidy as I would like it to be. I want to build on what I learn each day and check off my healing boxes as I would cross things off a to-do list. But that's not the way healing works. It's not linear. It is a journey of both progress and regress. And it's a daily battle not to be afraid in the midst of so many unknowns.

That's one of the myths I believed about healing for a long time. I thought I had to know how my future would play out in order to have the courage to walk out my healing journey. In short, I thought that God's vision for my future had to be aligned with *my* vision.

But now I know I had it backward. I needed to surrender my vision of what I wanted for God's better and more complete vision. That's what Jesus did in the garden of Gethsemane when he prayed: "'Abba, Father,' he said, 'everything is possible for you. Take this cup from me. Yet not what I will, but what you will'" (Mark 14:36).

Knowing what's up ahead is not really what I need most. And it's definitely not a prerequisite for healing. I think that's so important for you to know as we start this journey together in these pages.

Friend, no matter what unknowns or unanswered questions you woke up to today, let's find comfort in what we can absolutely count on from God today:

- God promises to guard your heart and mind (Philippians 4:6–7).
- God promises to give you His peace (John 14:27).
- God promises to comfort you in all your troubles (2 Corinthians 1:3–4).
- God promises to help you and strengthen you (Isaiah 41:10).
- God promises to bless, protect, and be gracious to you (Numbers 6:24–26).
- God promises to give you rest when you're weary and burdened (Matthew 11:28–30).
- God promises to hear and answer your prayers (1 John 5:14–15).
- God promises to supply all your needs (Philippians 4:19).

Jesus, who completely understands our desires for God to change the plans unfolding in front of us, came down to be the merciful and faithful High Priest modeling for us what to do when we face futures we fear. God has equipped us with the reassurance of His promises, His presence, and His perfect plan in the midst of a million imperfect realities. He thought of you when these verses were penned. And that thought of you flooded Him with a love so perfect, so complete, that He was willing to die so that you could truly live. He is the great love and the reassurance that your heart and mine are so desperately seeking.

His truth is the great love letter we get to read today. And tomorrow. And forever.

A statement to remember as I walk into today

God has a perfect plan in the midst of a million imperfect realities.

EVENING

My perspectives are limited.

So very limited.

When I forget this, I'm tempted to forget some of the promises from God that we read this morning.

I need God's perspectives to expand my own. Isaiah 55:9 reminds us, "As the heavens are higher than the earth, so are my ways higher than your ways and my thoughts than your thoughts."

Tonight, I'm making time to slow down and turn my focus to the Lord in prayer. And I'm asking for the humility to say, "God, please keep reminding me to not get attached to my own limited thinking. Give me eyes to see an expanded perspective beyond what I see right now."

Maybe for tonight—even for someone like me who craves certainty and answers—just a sliver is enough (Isaiah 46:10). Maybe for tonight, we can release what we think should happen and leave our hearts and minds open to hear from God.

We can rest tonight knowing He's not only got the whole world in His hands, but He's holding the details of our lives in His faithful hands as well. And everything His hands touch will eventually be redeemed.

Rest well.

SOMETHING TO RELEASE BACK TO GOD FROM TODAY:

_____

_____

A PRAYER TO RECEIVE BEFORE TOMORROW:

God, I am prone to forget Your faithful promises. Thank You for showing them to me in so many different Bible verses today. Thank You for caring about me and what I'm walking through. I trust You with what's heavy on my mind and know You see me as I lay those things down at Your feet tonight. In Jesus' name, amen.

DAY **2**

Living with the
Mystery

> Finally, brothers and sisters, whatever is true, whatever
> is noble, whatever is right, whatever is pure, whatever
> is lovely, whatever is admirable—if anything is excellent
> or praiseworthy—think about such things.
>
> PHILIPPIANS 4:8

MORNING

I read an interesting article while researching why my mind is so prone to run into the future and make predictions for my life. I'm also prone to bracing for impact by thinking through worst-case scenarios. I want to think about lovely and praiseworthy things, as Philippians 4:8 instructs, but my natural instincts make this incredibly difficult.

The article stated that our brains are wired for safety: "The brain is looking for ways to conserve energy and one way it does this is by making predictions so that we know what to expect and what the outcome of any given situation might be."[1] This helped me better understand why I am so resistant to living with unknowns and uncertainties. My brain is constantly searching for the reassurance of predictable safety, but none of us knows what's ahead. We can't clearly see what will happen in the next month, the next day, or even in the next hour.

Though this might be my brain's attempt to conserve energy, it makes my anxiety spiral. I've recently been learning how I can find security for today even as I face uncertainty about tomorrow. Rather than trying to predict the future, I trace God's faithfulness from my past. He was faithful then. He will be faithful now.

And I choose to remember how God gave me the strength to handle other hard circumstances, which reminds me He will most certainly give me what I need to handle this one.

I may not like all the circumstances from my past, but I can see I survived. God was with me. God has used parts of what I walked through for good. God used some of it to protect me. God has certainly used it to teach me lessons and make me more empathetic for others walking through hard things. And God has used some of it to position me for where I needed to be next.

There's still some mystery about some of what I've been through, but I can see God's faithfulness more clearly now than I did back then. I still don't have all the answers for why some of those things happened. But I can say with more certainty that faith helps make the most important fact known: the God who led me to this will surely help me through this. Nothing has ever caught God by surprise. Not in your life or mine. The evils done to us break His heart, but how we will survive them is not a mystery to God. This insight can help us not feel so panicked with the uncertainties for the future.

So how do we handle the uncertainties of today? We stick close to God. Our job is to be obedient to God. God's job is everything else.

I can find security for today even as I face uncertainty about tomorrow.

EVENING

Another thing that confuses me and stirs up my anxiety is when things seem to be harder and harder for me, while someone who hurt me appears to be thriving. I feel like I'm trying to be obedient to God, so shouldn't I be the one who is thriving?

How can the one who keeps on sinning seem so happy and without care in the world? God, do You see me at all?

Have you experienced this?

This seems unfair. But remember, we don't know the full story of what's really happening with that other person. Just because something looks good doesn't mean that it is good. The same fire that provides warmth can also severely burn you. The same water that feels refreshing can be a destructive flood. The same sin that brings someone temporary pleasure can be a regret that leaves permanent scars.

Remember that sin is always a package deal of both tempting pleasures and eventual consequences. If someone participates in the pleasures, they will absolutely unleash the resulting consequences. You may not see the consequence of another person's sin, but you can know it's there.

Our job isn't to focus on the other person's sin and consequences. We must focus our attention on processing and healing from what hurt us. We must work through what we've walked through. If we don't, we may risk lashing out from our unhealed places.

We must keep trusting God's faithfulness and obeying God's instructions during this healing journey. We may not know what tomorrow holds, but we can be confident in the God who holds all our tomorrows.

SOMETHING TO RELEASE BACK TO GOD FROM TODAY:

_____

_____

A PRAYER TO RECEIVE BEFORE TOMORROW:

Lord, thank You for anchoring me in the middle of the unknowns I am facing. Even when I long for certainty and control, help me remember my job today is to stay focused on what You are asking me to do, and You will take care of the rest. I love You. In Jesus' name, amen.

DAY

3

Embracing Today's Grace Even When I Don't Feel Grateful

> Therefore do not worry about tomorrow, for tomorrow will worry about itself. Each day has enough trouble of its own.
>
> MATTHEW 6:34

MORNING

Sometimes being grateful means choosing to see what is instead of being blinded by what isn't. It's a tough choice in some moments. Brutal, actually. But it's worth fighting through.

Even now, I have days where what is missing in my life feels like a huge, gaping hole. Everywhere I look, it feels like the hole is the center of my vision staring me in the face.

But then I stop, and I shift my focus. I roll up my sleeves, and I roll out some cookie dough with my granddaughters. I direct my gaze off that hole. I intentionally redirect my focus to these little girls' precious faces and this priceless moment right in front of me. And I'm once again reminded that there is so much more to this one incredible life than the sum total of our heartbreak.

We can thank God for the gift of this day. Enjoy the mess out of today. Receive the blessing of this day. Dance it out at least one time today. Fill in the gaps with prayer throughout the day. And make it a goal to go to bed with a smile on your face because of today. Because here's what I know: God gives us "today" grace.

We should carry only what we must on this day. Then tomorrow, we will have tomorrow's grace. And six months from now, the grace for that day will greet us and help us carry the weight of that day.

Where I sometimes get in trouble is trying to carry today's stress with tomorrow's worry and the fear of six months from now all with today's grace. That's when it all feels like too much to bear.

It's not that we don't want to plan for the future and be discerning about how to handle what's next responsibly. That's wise and good.

It's just that we don't want to become so stressed, fearful, and full of anxiety about tomorrow that we miss the grace and goodness of this beautiful day.

So today, receive both the grace and the gifts of this day. Don't miss one minute of its unexpected treasure, and celebrate every bit of its joy.

God gives us "today" grace.

EVENING

Choosing gratitude right in the middle of what's hard isn't denial. But it is choosing to do only what can be done today.

For me, choosing gratitude might look like doing what can be done that day—and then going to play in the sand with my amazing grandkids on a warm afternoon that is full of smiles, North Carolina blue skies, and a crazy amount of washed-up seashells.

Maybe gratitude isn't something we have to contain within ourselves. Maybe it's something we experience and express right in the middle of it all.

And that's what makes it sweet (and salty from all the sand I'm currently covered in from being the Gigi who offered to pioneer sandcastle making today).

Before you go to sleep tonight, consider releasing that feeling that what's currently hard or challenging is the sum total of your life right now. Ask God to help you exchange this for a different perspective.

SOMETHING TO RELEASE BACK TO GOD FROM TODAY:

_____

_____

A PRAYER TO RECEIVE BEFORE TOMORROW:

Dear Lord, You made me. You know me. I need Your help where I am weak. Help me see that even the smallest moments really do contain opportunities for gratitude. Give me the courage and the grace to do what pleases You. I want to do Your will and experience more of You in this season. In Jesus' name, amen.

DAY 4

The
Uncomfortable
Quiet

> You will keep in perfect peace those whose minds
> are steadfast, because they trust in you.
>
> ISAIAH 26:3

MORNING

I had a meeting with my counselor recently where I wanted to process my loneliness. I've never lived alone in all fifty-two years of my life. I grew up with sisters. I went to college and always had roommates. I got married and then had five children.

My house went from feeling full of noise and other people for decades to being suddenly, shockingly quiet. The kids are now grown. And the marriage I thought would last a lifetime ended after continuous broken trust and betrayal.

I'd spent years focused on raising the kids, working in ministry, and trying to repair and save what eventually proved to be an unsustainable relationship.

When the shocking discoveries were hitting me over and over for years, I begged God for all the chaos to stop. Eventually, it did. But then, the quietness of the aftermath slammed into my life. I imagine it is similar to the quietness after a tornado has ripped through a community. Or to the eerie feeling after a house fire. The damage from the trauma is most apparent after the source of the trauma leaves.

That's when you see the real impact of the loss.

It's a lot to take in, and most of the time it will take years to fully process.

I wasn't lonely at first. There were more immediate emotions to work through in the quiet. I feel like I've cycled through the shock, the sadness, the anger, the disillusionment, and the fear. Now it's the loneliness that seems to be most front and center. It's uncomfortable in some of the better moments but can easily intensify to a panicked uncertainty about the future.

My counselor has encouraged me to learn to sit in the quietness and loneliness and not rush to fill it. Though I don't like this answer, I know he's right. I need to reflect. I need to learn the complicated but exquisite beauty of being honest about what is and what is not acceptable. I need to rediscover who God created me to be and not who someone else's issues demanded I be. I need time to work on my own issues. I need to grow, learn, mature.

Most of all I need to reset what is and is not normal. When you've lived a long time with the dysfunctions of unacceptable behaviors, these can seem more and more normal. I need to establish a new normal for myself.

So in the quiet, I turn toward God and the goodness He intends for my life from here. And I take one more quiet step toward healing.

Here's what I've found. Sometimes "quiet" is the beginning of an anthem song called "resilience."

God is in the quiet. Lonely is His invitation away from distraction.

After several times of sitting with God in the quiet, I stood in front of the mirror and said,

"I will get up."

"I will trust God."

"I will get healthy."

"I will get strong."

"I will get prepared."

"This isn't an ending."

"Every great start begins with a stop."

Oh, friend. Would you make space to sit in the quiet for a moment this morning and just listen? Even in the tension of it all? The questions, the crippling anxieties, the fears. All of it.

Right where you are, open your hands and tell God you're listening.

Because here's what I know: He's listening too. Every single word within every single prayer you've prayed? He's heard you.

Psalm 5:3 says, "In the morning, LORD, you hear my voice; in the morning I lay my requests before you and wait expectantly."

I love that verse. But notice how there's a few different components. The first part talks about active prayer where we bring our requests to the Lord. Then there are two words at the end that really catch my attention: *wait expectantly.*

That's what I think making room for the quiet invites us to do.

While we sit in the quiet, we wait expectantly. We can listen. Grieve. Learn. Heal. And walk forward knowing that because of God, whatever was meant for harm only served to make us more capable.

Not less.

I think you're resilient. And I know healing is possible today. So don't be afraid of the quiet; God is right there. Make the decision to unrush your mind. Let His still, small voice start to uncomplicate your heart. He will be there to comfort you every step of the way today.

P.S. The song "Quiet" (the stripped-down version) by Elevation Worship has been one of my favorite songs in this season. Give it a listen!

Don't be afraid of the quiet; God is right there.

EVENING

Sometimes the quietness of the evening is more complicated and painful than during the day. I think this can be true even if your home is still full of people, but there's a sense of sadness or loss that you're carrying in your heart. I'm learning I have a choice for what to do in the uncomfortable quiet.

I can fill it with thoughts of worst-case scenarios and fears. Or I can use this time to reflect, pray, and lead my alarming thoughts to more peaceful thoughts of gratitude. I can practice self-care, and I can read books that help me learn and grow. I love the reminder we find in Isaiah 30:15: "This is what the Sovereign Lord, the Holy One of Israel, says: 'In repentance and rest is your salvation, in quietness and trust is your strength.'"

I want the outcome of this uncomfortable quiet to be the time in my life where I learned to trust God more than ever—which will make this a season of newfound strength.

Isn't it the loveliest thought that God might be waiting for there to be some silence in our lives to share some of His best secrets with us?

The Enemy wants us to believe that times of silence are a curse of loneliness. A burden of shame. A reminder of the remains of what once was but is no longer. But God wants us to know that times of silence are really pathways to closeness with Him.

I know the quiet can sometimes be deafeningly loud. But as you go to sleep tonight, I want you to think about what an invitation this sacred silence could be and what could be possible because of it.

Release the lies keeping you from leaning into what God may have for you here, in the quiet. Sweet dreams, friend.

SOMETHING TO RELEASE BACK TO GOD FROM TODAY:

_____

_____

Lord, when I start to feel anxious during the quiet, I invite You into those moments. I pray that You would speak to me in the still moments and that I would learn to listen to Your voice. Thank You for helping me heal and keep pressing into You during this journey. In Jesus' name, amen.

DAY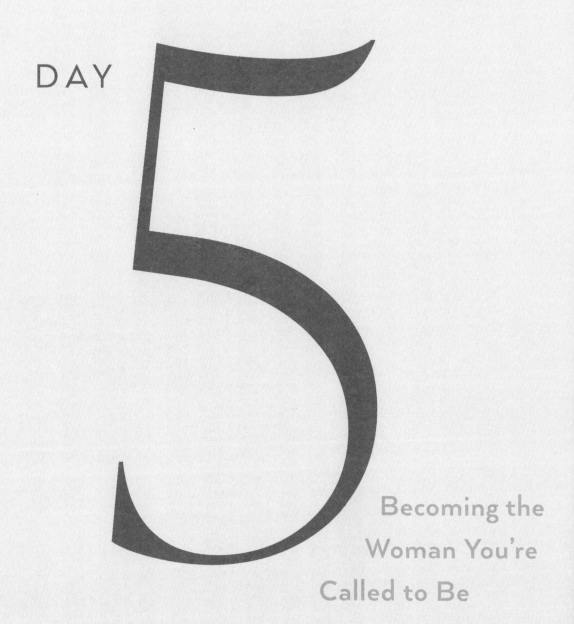

5

Becoming the
Woman You're
Called to Be

> Whoever walks in integrity walks securely.
>
> PROVERBS 10:9

MORNING

One night recently, my kids came over and we spent hours looking at and laughing over hundreds of pictures in our family scrapbooks.

Decades of memories.

I was surprised I didn't get triggered. But I didn't. And I think it's because I've been working hard not to let what is heartbreaking right now steal the memories from years past that are so precious to me.

I felt empowered to own what was all so true to me. I was authentically present, loving these memory-making moments with my kids.

Everything wasn't picture-perfect. Some of the most hilarious moments were because of imperfections, bad attitudes, and vacation details gone bad. But it was delightful to laugh

through our shared experiences. There was a sense of belonging because we knew our inside jokes, quirks, and stories.

I loved it. And it made me strengthen my commitment to walk into this next season of life being a woman my kids can count on and be proud of.

I think about what I want the most sacred and precious moments of my life to look like, and I must continue to make decisions today that stay in line with that. I must model the character I've taught my kids to have.

I'm sure I'll make mistakes; we all do. But I can choose to make the patterns of my life line up with God's truth by doing what the Bible instructs, prioritizing emotional health, and being someone my people can trust.

I want to sleep well at night knowing I never traded my integrity for shortsighted pleasure. The Bible tells us in Proverbs 10:9, "Whoever walks in integrity walks securely." I don't know about you, but I love that word *securely*. When you're in the middle of something hard or even trying to heal and move forward, the process is messy and uncertain. The road ahead feels long and unpredictable. But in the middle of that, we get to choose to walk in integrity, which brings about the security we desperately want.

Wow.

I may not know how every detail of my story will play out. But here's what I do know: when the sun is setting on my last day here, I want to be surrounded by my people recalling all our best moments together. That's joy. That's purpose. That's a life well lived. That's what it's all about.

Won't you join me, friend? What is a choice you could make with integrity today?

No matter where you've been or what has happened to you, today is a great day to start becoming the woman you know you're called to be. Come on, friend. Let's do this. Let's do this right. I believe in you. Today is the best day to start.

A statement to remember as I walk into today:

We get to choose to walk in integrity, which brings about the security we desperately want.

Some people say time heals all wounds. But I don't agree.

We need to release the thought that things will naturally get better on their own. We need to seek God. We need to get the appropriate help and support. And we need to humbly receive truth every day.

I think it's what we plant in the soil of that time that determines what we yield.

Oh, friend. I see who you're becoming. You're planting wisely. I mean, look at what you're choosing to spend your time doing right now. You are positioning your heart in the direction of truth because you want godly wisdom.

You're leaning in.

You're processing.

You're praying.

You're grieving.

You're worshiping.

You're healing.

You're planting wisely.

I know it can be hard to figure out this whole healing thing. I understand. I agree.

But I just wanted to remind you tonight that you're not alone.

You're going to make it.

Actually, and even better, we're going to make it *together*.

SOMETHING TO RELEASE BACK TO GOD FROM TODAY:

_____

_____

A PRAYER TO RECEIVE BEFORE TOMORROW:

Jesus, I want to be a woman full of integrity. I want to be someone my family is proud of and—more important—someone You are proud of. Help me continue to plant wisely during this healing journey. Thank You for sustaining me on the days I feel like I can't keep going. I love You, Lord. In Jesus' name, amen.

DAY

6

But They
Seem to
Get Away
with Everything

> "In your anger do not sin": Do not let the sun go down while you are still angry, and do not give the devil a foothold.... Get rid of all bitterness, rage and anger, brawling and slander, along with every form of malice.
>
> EPHESIANS 4:26–27, 31

MORNING

I was sitting in the sand watching the salty water inch closer and closer. The tide was coming in, and I knew if I didn't move, the water would soon wash over me and my stuff. The beauty of the ocean comes with the reality of the tide.

Many things in life come as a package deal like this. When we choose to participate with part of it, we participate with all of it. Relationships are this way. Jobs are this way. Owning a home is this way. Even vacations are this way.

All these things are package deals—they come with fun parts and hard parts. And sin is no different. Like we talked about the other day—whatever seems enticing about the sin will always come with the consequences of that sin.

When other people sin against us, intentionally wrong us, and blatantly hurt us but never seem to have consequences for any of it, this apparent lack of fairness is what stirs up feelings of bitterness, unforgiveness, and even retaliation. But it's crucial that we don't let these feelings that come at us get inside of us.

The truth that helps me manage the "unfairness" of hurtful situations is remembering that when people sin against us, they unleash into their lives the consequences of that sin. We may never see it. In fact, it may look like they just got away with everything. But today we can be reminded that eventually "they will eat the fruit of their ways and be filled with the fruit of their schemes" (Proverbs 1:31).

The best thing we can do is trust God with their consequences while making sure we don't get lured into sinful choices resulting from our own bitterness and unforgiveness.

Friend, your heart is much too beautiful of a place to be tainted by hurt, haunted by resentment, or held back by bitterness. It's time to stop suffering because of what another person has done to you. And maybe holding firmly to this perspective is just one of the many ways God wants to help us heal today.

Your heart is much too beautiful of a place to be tainted by hurt, haunted by resentment, or held back by bitterness.

EVENING

Many times throughout the Bible where there is a warning about unforgiveness, there is also a warning about the schemes and temptations of the Enemy. In 2 Corinthians 2:10–11, the apostle Paul stated, "I have forgiven in the sight of Christ for your sake, in order that Satan might not outwit us. For we are not unaware of his schemes." Then in Ephesians 4:26–27, Paul wrote, "'In your anger do not sin': Do not let the sun go down while you are still angry, and do not give the devil a foothold." Paul continued this thought in verse 31 with his instructions to "get rid of all bitterness, rage and anger, brawling and slander, along with every form of malice."

When we feel bitterness, we must call it what it really is. It's not something that protects us from not getting hurt again. It's not something that hurts the person who hurt us. It is the very place where the Enemy can lure us into his schemes and where we can be so very tempted to sin.

Oh, friend. Never forget your position of strength isn't anger, bitterness, or retaliation. It's humility.

When we are humble, it doesn't mean we are bowing down in defeat. It means we are rising up to declare that no one has the power to make us betray who we really are in Christ. We can stand up for what is right, have hard conversations, and even confront things that need to be addressed in equal measures of grace and truth—and we can do all this without losing the best of who we are in the process.

Tonight, let's release those feelings of anger by acknowledging to God that when we feel hurt, it doesn't mean we have to live lives that perpetuate that hurt. We may need to work through those feelings, but we do not need to let our lives be hijacked by those feelings.

SOMETHING TO RELEASE BACK TO GOD FROM TODAY:

_____

_____

Father God, today I bring my difficult relationship situations to You. I know You see me struggle and have not left me to figure this out on my own. When unforgiveness, bitterness, resentment, and judgment rise up in my heart, please help me process those feelings in a healthy way. In Jesus' name, amen.

DAY 7

When It May Be Time to Draw a Healthy Boundary

Like a city whose walls are broken through is a person who lacks self-control.

PROVERBS 25:28

MORNING

I'll never forget asking my counselor to help me process how I finally got to the place where I said, "No more. No more devastation. No more betrayal. No more being lied to. No more."

I wondered if that was the moment I became broken. But he replied, "No, Lysa, that was the moment you declared you were healing."

Sometimes "no more" means implementing good boundaries that will help hold each person accountable to healthier relational patterns. Sometimes "no more" means acknowledging a heartbreaking reality that wise counsel has helped you see is no longer sustainable.

Both dynamics require that we pursue healing. We need solid truth from God's Word to help guide and direct us. Sometimes we may need a godly professional counselor who is trained to educate, comfort, and challenge us.

I know what it feels like to be paralyzed by another person's choices and not know what to do about it. In the past, I've been hesitant to draw boundaries because it felt uncaring and because I didn't have the confidence to know how to implement and communicate healthy parameters.

Now I've discovered a better way to view boundaries. I don't draw boundaries hoping to force another person to change in ways they may be unwilling or incapable of changing. Instead, I place boundaries on myself to help me exercise self-control over what I will and will not tolerate. Self-control is crucial so that I regulate my reactions and direct my efforts toward keeping myself in a healthy place.

Good boundaries are the only fighting chance we have for navigating relational challenges in a productive and healthy way.

If you're in a "no more" kind of place, consider these questions about boundaries and how you might be able to apply this in your own life beginning today.

- What kind of person do I want to be, not just in this relationship but consistently in all of my relationships?
- What do I need to do in this relationship to stay consistent in my character, conduct, and communication?
- What are some areas of my life in which I have the most limited capacity? (Example: at my job, in parenting, during the holidays, and so forth.)

- Based on my realistic assessment of capacity, how does this relationship threaten to hyperextend what I can realistically and even generously give?
- Do I feel the freedom in this relationship to communicate what I can and cannot give without the fear of being punished or pushed away?
- What are some realistic restrictions I can place on myself to reduce the access this person has to my most limited emotional or physical resources?
- In what ways is this person's unpredictable behavior negatively impacting my trust in my other relationships?
- How am I suffering the consequences of their choices more than they are?
- What are this person's most realistic and most unrealistic expectations of me? What are my most realistic and most unrealistic expectations of this person?
- What boundaries do I need to put in place?

As you consider these questions, you may find it helpful to process them with a trusted godly mentor or Christian counselor. These questions to consider aren't to complicate our relational dynamics further; they are meant to help identify where we are dancing with dysfunction. Toxic realities in relationships will not tame themselves. We cannot ignore them into health. And we can't badger them into a better place. We must get honest about the hardships that are complicating and probably preventing the kind of health we not only want but *need* for some of our relationships to survive.

I've learned we can't just "get over" our hurts. And boundaries are a great way to start experiencing health in your own life today.

A statement to remember as I walk into today:

Good boundaries are the only fighting chance we have for navigating relational challenges in a productive and healthy way.

EVENING

As I've processed how to draw some necessary boundaries in my own life, something my counselor has reminded me over and over again is, "We train people how to treat us." Now, please don't hear that harshly. If you're in an abusive situation, this isn't meant to make you think you've brought this on yourself. And if you've suffered emotional trauma in a relationship, this doesn't mean you could have done something to prevent it. But it is important for us all to know, moving forward, that we get to verbalize what is and is not acceptable in the context of relationships. Please see page 209 for information on resources that might help you.

I'm challenging myself with all this. Friend, let's remember that what we allow is what we will live. I don't want us living anything that's not biblical or possible to endure. Maybe it's time to retrain some people in our lives with clearly stated, gracefully implemented, and consistently kept boundaries.

It's for the sake of your sanity that you draw necessary boundaries. It's for the sake of stability that you stay consistent with those boundaries.

Setting healthy boundaries is absolutely necessary for true freedom, growth, and healing to take place. Boundaries aren't meant to shove the other person away; they're to keep yourself together. And boundaries enable you to continue to love that person and treat them with respect without losing the best of who you are.

I've seen progress in some of my most challenging relationships because of boundaries. And I want this for you, too, friend.

SOMETHING TO RELEASE BACK TO GOD FROM TODAY:

_____

_____

A PRAYER TO RECEIVE BEFORE TOMORROW:

God, I need Your help to consider areas in my life where I may need to implement healthy boundaries. Help me to process these decisions thoroughly, through the lens of wisdom and with godly counsel. I long to see health in all my relationships, so help me see where boundaries could make this possible. I want to honor You in my relationships. In Jesus' name, amen.

DAY

8

You Don't
Have to
Live Lonely

> Oil and perfume make the heart glad, and the sweetness
> of a friend comes from his earnest counsel.
>
> PROVERBS 27:9 ESV

MORNING

Have you ever felt utterly alone even in a room full of people? I understand.

Feeling left out and lonely isn't something that's reserved only for playground games and middle school dances. I've still felt that same sense of loneliness even as an adult.

No matter how you feel this morning, I want you to let this truth, God's truth, surround you in a symphony of compassion and comfort: *you are not alone.*

You may feel lonely, but you don't have to live lonely.

So, what can you do? You can refuse to isolate. It can be tempting to look at others on social media laughing, connecting, and cheering one another on and make assumptions. It's easy to assume that they don't struggle with loneliness. It's easy to assume that you don't fit in or belong. It's easy to assume that the world just seems to be moving on without you. All those assumptions will exhaust you and tempt you to isolate even more. Isolation is never a cure for your longing for real connection. I believe the most powerful cure for loneliness can be found in one of my favorite words: *togetherness*. Togetherness reminds us we are all so very human and united in our laughter, tears, love for Jesus, and tender care for one another.

So, I have a challenge for you today.

Do you have a friend in your life who speaks truth? Listen to her. Stay connected to her. Let her lead you back to God time and time again. Because just like the breaking of bread sustains our physical bodies, breaking secrecy with trusted friends nourishes the deep places in our souls.

And if you don't have that kind of friend, ask God for this gift. In the meantime, I hope, in some small way, I'm that kind of friend for you here in the pages of this devotional book.

Together is such a beautiful thing. I pray today God gives you an opportunity to pursue togetherness with safe people . . . because chances are that you'll be a blessing to them in their lonely feelings as well.

A statement to remember as I walk into today:

You may feel lonely, but you don't have to live lonely.

EVENING

Sometimes it can be hard to make friends. It takes time to form deep connections and build the kind of trust where a friendship feels safe and stable. If you're struggling because of a move or a recent friendship breakup, or maybe your life circumstances have changed and created a disconnect with those you used to have more in common with, those struggles are real.

I understand how that feels.

But here's what I want you to remember before you go to sleep tonight: *you are loved.* You may feel the stinging pain of loneliness, but you are not alone. The God of the universe knows you, accepts you, and loves you right where you are. Remembering this may not fix the ways you feel left out, but it does remind you who you are.

You are extremely loved, friend. Rest tonight in the promise of that.

Pray that God shows you someone else who needs a friend, and tomorrow, make it a point to reach out to her.

SOMETHING TO RELEASE BACK TO GOD FROM TODAY:

_____

_____

A PRAYER TO RECEIVE BEFORE TOMORROW:

God, I know You often work in ways I don't understand. Even when I feel lonely, I trust You are making something beautiful even out of these parts of my life that sting with hurt, pain, and grief. I pray for opportunities to pursue togetherness with other believers who are also committed to following You. In Jesus' name, amen.

DAY

Maybe We're
All More Alike
Than We Thought

> So in everything, do to others what you would have them do
> to you, for this sums up the Law and the Prophets.
>
> MATTHEW 7:12

MORNING

I wonder if one of the reasons we can sometimes feel overwhelmingly lonely is because we live in a world so full of division. And while we won't always understand everyone else's thoughts, opinions, and ways of processing life, we *can* focus on areas where we are all more alike than different.

We all have tearstains on our pillows and have faced:

Unforeseeable life-altering circumstances . . .
Unresolved relationship tensions . . .
Unanswered prayer requests . . .

When our hearts get broken, it hurts. Grief stings. Hard stuff piled on top of hard stuff is disorienting for all of us.

It seems we are all carrying a bit of sorrow or frustration or heaviness these days. And when we take time to remember this, compassion grows in our hearts toward others because the reality is, they're hurting too. Maybe the truth that we're all carrying some form of pain in our hearts means we're a lot more alike than we are different. Today is a great day to reach out with compassion to another hurting human soul.

Make that phone call.
Send that card you wish you would receive today.
Leave that encouraging comment on her social media.
Stop by just to say hello with her favorite coffee.
Pray more words over her and refuse to talk about her.
Pick a flower and place it where she can see something beautiful today.
Give a friend a pinwheel and take a photo of the two of you proving life isn't all bad.

We are so very united in our struggles. We are so very united in our tears.
Jesus, help us remember this today. And even more importantly, help us live this today.

A statement to remember as I walk into today:

Today is a great day to reach out with compassion to another hurting human soul.

EVENING

One of the most compassionate things we can do for others is create a space where they know they're welcome just as they are. Around a table. On a walk. Maybe even a road trip. Initiating those moments where togetherness says, "You belong. You have a place. You have a voice. You have people. You are loved."

When you're hurting, it can feel isolating when you aren't sure how to talk about the hard things or who can safely hold your honest thoughts. But compassion allows us to love people who are hurting, empathize with their pain, and acknowledge their side of things, even if we can't change the outcome or fix things for them.

Only God can do that.

But what *can* we do? Show up. Invite. Initiate. Comfort. Pray. Release our desire to control things or change people and just simply create space for the Holy Spirit to move.

We can show up with Jesus in our hearts and compassion in our words and just be there.

Who is someone in your life who may need to be reminded of this tonight? Maybe shoot that person a quick text saying, "Hey, friend. Jesus loves you, and I love you, and I'm here for you."

And if you're that person who needs to be reminded she's a little less alone in what she's walking through right now, I'll be that friend for you.

Hey, you. Jesus loves you, and today isn't the whole story. Keep going. You're going to make it. Sweet dreams.

SOMETHING TO RELEASE BACK TO GOD FROM TODAY:

_____

_____

A PRAYER TO RECEIVE BEFORE TOMORROW:

Father God, sometimes I forget we all have tearstains on our pillows. Keep reminding me that every person I come across needs compassion. And I might be the only one in their lives right now who has the chance to help and the courage to care. In Jesus' name, amen.

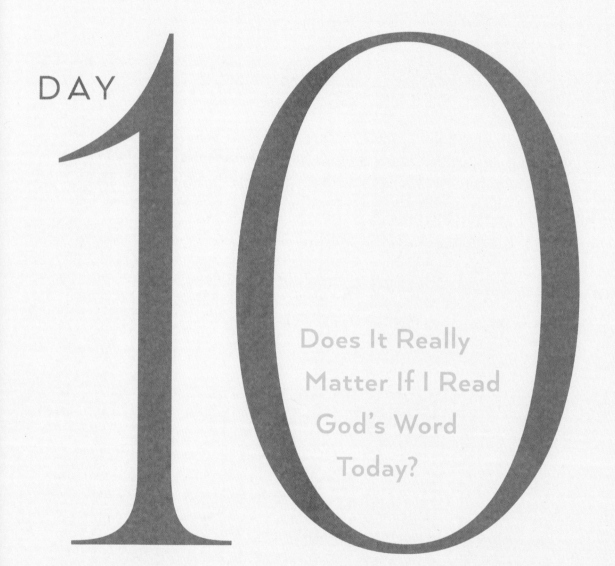

DAY

10

Does It Really
Matter If I Read
God's Word
Today?

> So is my word that goes out from my mouth: It will not return to me empty,
> but will accomplish what I desire and achieve the purpose for which I sent it.
>
> ISAIAH 55:11

MORNING

Do you ever feel overwhelmed when you sit down to read your Bible?

Me too . . . especially when hurtful situations leave me worn out and worn down, unmotivated to spend time with God.

When we're in these desperate places, it's easy to want God to rain down "right now" wisdom full of immediate answers and solutions for what's breaking our hearts. But spending time in God's Word offers us so much more than quick fixes. You see, the Bible doesn't just give us instruction for today—it also plants wisdom in our hearts for the future.

How? Well, God already sees everything coming our way, and that means He knows exactly how to begin preparing our hearts today for tomorrow.

I've seen this to be true in my own life.

Recently, I was at a women's gathering where I was about to walk on the stage and study the Bible with others. And just minutes before, I got a call that sent my anxiety soaring. The tightness in my chest quickly gave way to a flood of tears. The news absolutely devastated me, but I had an assignment before me.

So I took a deep breath.

I wiped my tears.

I whispered the one shred of truth I could remember from Bible verses that had been on repeat in my mind: *God is faithful. He is living water for my soul.* (Isaiah 55:10–11; John 7:38; John 4:13–14).

Then I turned to my friends who were with me and said, "This is what it looks like to walk in the strength of the Lord. Never forget this. He is always faithful." I stepped into studying Scripture and was astounded by the power of the Holy Spirit that poured out over our gathering.

I don't tell you this to highlight my own strength, because frankly, I didn't feel like I had much at that moment. But if you're asking yourself, *Does it really matter if I read God's Word today?,* remember that storing Scripture deep in our hearts prepares us for the unpredictable moments. The unforeseeable circumstances. The moments that take our breath away, leaving us no other option but to trust God to carry us through.

I have found in my own life, the days I feel like opening God's Word the least are the days I need God's Word the most.

Let's open God's Word today. Whether you feel like it or you're not sure you can, even if it's just one or two verses, read Scripture. You can start with the passages I mentioned above. Or go to one of your old favorites. More than just reading His words, we must choose to receive them. Even more important, we must live them.

The more we apply God's teaching to our lives, the more it becomes part of us. For today. For one day. For every day.

A statement to remember as I walk into today:

The days I feel like opening God's Word the least are the days I need God's Word the most.

EVENING

Our commitment to meditating on God's Word shouldn't be limited to a morning discipline. It's also a beautiful exercise to do right before we go to sleep. When we're going through something challenging and are tempted to fall asleep thinking about all the hard things, God's Word directs our hearts and minds toward healing truths.

Here are some verses to start with for tonight:

- "In God, whose word I praise—in God I trust and am not afraid. What can mere mortals do to me?" (Psalm 56:4).
- "He sent out his word and healed them, and delivered them from their destruction" (Psalm 107:20 ESV).
- "In peace I will both lie down and sleep; for you alone, O LORD, make me dwell in safety" (Psalm 4:8 ESV).

If I could go back and gently encourage my younger self in a desperate season, I would remind myself of something my friend Kimberly Henderson told me one day about God's Word: "Some days God's Word is going to feed us right away like bread, and other days it might feel more like holding on to seeds. Words that we may not grasp why we need them just yet still should be deposited in our hearts so they can grow."

_____

_____

A PRAYER TO RECEIVE BEFORE TOMORROW:

Jesus, on the days I'm tempted to cut out time spent in Your Word, remind me of what I've read today. Time spent in Your Word is never wasted. Thank You for the way Your words provide direction, instruction, and wisdom both for today and for the future. In Jesus' name, amen.

DAY

11

Having
All the
Answers
Isn't What
I Need
Most

> "I have told you these things, so that in me you may
> have peace. In this world you will have trouble. But
> take heart! I have overcome the world."
>
> JOHN 16:33

MORNING

I've been studying the life of Jesus a lot. How He reacted when people hurt Him deeply. How He handled the whiplash of being loved one minute and tossed aside the next. How He stayed peaceful but also sometimes got "overwhelmed with sorrow" (Mark 14:34). How He knew Judas was going to betray Him, and He washed his feet anyhow.

And I'm learning a lot.

When I desperately want to know why, I remember that Jesus had all the answers, and He still wept (John 11:35).

So, maybe having the answers for why hurt happens wouldn't be as comforting as I always thought it would be.

Maybe not understanding is what grows our faith. Maybe being too full of answers is what slows our faith.

In the end, I think that when we go through stuff, it's an opportunity to be the purest reflection of Jesus.

This is my greatest desire. I won't do it perfectly. But I will pursue doing it wholeheartedly.

Sometimes God has to lean in close to our hearts full of questions and gently whisper, *You don't have to have all the answers. You just need to trust.*

What could this look like for you today? Could you shift from asking why something hard is happening to you to asking God how He wants to use this for you? Or, maybe, just simply stand outside today, and as you look up and realize the sky isn't falling and you are still breathing, release your *why* questions to God, trusting Him to carry the reasons. Then imagine Him holding your hand as you keep walking forward.

Sometimes God has to lean in close to our hearts full of questions and gently whisper, "You don't have to have all the answers. You just need to trust."

EVENING

When we're in the middle of wrestling with God through our questions, it's easy to feel like He's left us alone to figure it all out. But friend, even in things we don't understand, He's here with us right now.

God isn't intimidated by your questions. He is present in the middle of them. And God isn't hiding His goodness from you. He wants you to see His goodness as you keep trusting Him.

What *why* questions do you want to release to God this evening, so you don't have to keep getting bogged down by their burden? After all, even if you had those answers today, chances are that knowing *why* wouldn't make the pain go away and may never make sense to you anyhow.

SOMETHING TO RELEASE BACK TO GOD FROM TODAY:

_____

_____

A PRAYER TO RECEIVE BEFORE TOMORROW:

Lord, thank You for who Jesus is—one who deeply understands how hard it can be to wrestle with the why questions as a human. Thank You for the truth that, when I'm praying, You hear me. You will carry the reasons this happened because only You know what to do with those. And You will carry me. Because Jesus has overcome the world, I know You will help me overcome what I'm facing as well. I love You, Lord. In Jesus' name, amen.

DAY

12

Looking for
Beautiful
When It's
Hard to
Find

> "See, I am doing a new thing! Now it springs up; do you not perceive it? I am making a way in the wilderness and streams in the wasteland."
>
> ISAIAH 43:19

MORNING

Part of learning to see beautiful again is recognizing that a hard season doesn't mean that every day has to be hard.

Sorrow and celebration can coexist. As a matter of fact, I think they should coexist. There's still beauty to be found in the ashes (Isaiah 61:3). Joy can be found in the midst of hardship, and peace can exist in the middle of unresolved conflict.

And there are still so many reasons to celebrate and thank God.

That doesn't mean we throw a party and fake our way through a celebration. But it does mean despite the pain of the hurt, we can intentionally find something to celebrate in the midst of today's sorrow. I want to remind you today that this is possible so you don't miss it.

- Listen to that song—the one where you can't stay down when its rhythm gets turned all the way up.
- Dance. Sing. Let go for a moment.
- Watch something funny with a friend and remember how good it feels to laugh.
- Stand in front of the ocean or a lake and remember how big the world really is. There are new joys to discover and enjoy and, yes, celebrate.

God has beauty in store for us today. We just need to be intentional about looking for it. Let's ask God to show it to us today. Let's believe it's already there for us to find.

And when you're not feeling brave, say this: "I'm so much stronger than I ever dreamed possible. And when I'm not, God still is. Thank You, God. Help me, God. Show me, God."

Find the beauty today. I just know it's waiting to be found by you.

A statement to remember as I walk into today:

A hard season doesn't mean that every day has to be hard.

Do you need a reminder of what seeing beautiful again looks like?

Seeing beautiful again is that flicker of unexplainable peace. It's a reminder that this big and sometimes scary world still has the touch of God on it and the presence of God in it. Where God is, beautiful can be found.

When I see beautiful, I try to capture it with words or a picture.

It's deciding to carry a fun colored umbrella into the rainiest of days. It's noticing the yellow sun saying goodbye to this day by blowing kisses of orange and pink. It's walking across a

wooden bridge and seeing the unexpected gorgeous colors of the marsh catching me by surprise. It's realizing how much intentionality God puts in the smallest details in nature and knowing He's just as intentional with a good plan for my life as well.

Seeing beautiful is intentionally remembering the goodness and faithfulness of God.

It's a moment that feels right even when other things don't. It's a summer breeze, key lime pie, and ordering mac and cheese on a whim because it reminds me of something good and right from my childhood.

Seeing beautiful is a Scripture verse that settles into my soul and a prayer that settles me down. It's hearing a song that captures what I feel in lyrics and a chorus with a really great beat.

It's saying, "We're going to make it through this together." And then you do.

Can I whisper something to you before you go to sleep tonight?

Beautiful is there in your life too.

Sometimes it just takes noticing it to finally be delighted and comforted by it. Remember, God created beautiful, and He is delighted when we notice it. I believe there is still beautiful in your life, and God is waiting each day for you to experience it, friend.

SOMETHING TO RELEASE BACK TO GOD FROM TODAY:

_____

_____

A PRAYER TO RECEIVE BEFORE TOMORROW:

Lord, I believe You see things I cannot see, so give me the courage to press in even when I'm struggling to see what You are doing in my life. I know You are always doing more than what I can see right away, and I trust You with all my heart. Help me see all the beauty You've placed in my life even in unexpected and unlikely places. In Jesus' name, amen.

DAY 13

Planting Small
Seeds That Reap
Big Rewards

He told them another parable: "The kingdom of heaven is like a mustard seed, which a man took and planted in his field. Though it is the smallest of all seeds, yet when it grows, it is the largest of garden plants and becomes a tree, so that the birds come and perch in its branches."

MATTHEW 13:31-32

MORNING

Isn't it easy to overlook small opportunities to help others because we don't think it would make a real difference?

Little acts of kindness, chances to help another person, will pass us right by if we're not carefully paying attention.

These things might seem meaningless, but when we get to heaven, I think we will be surprised by what mattered the most. What actually changed the world. What fulfilled the purposes for which we were created.

The small places we showed up and served in obedience will prompt Jesus to say, "Well done. Remember when you took the time to share encouraging words with someone who needed it? That's the day you helped change the world."

But I also know when you feel unseen, unheard, and unnoticed, it can feel incredibly hard to muster up encouraging words for others.

Let's not overlook the small opportunities where we can invest in others—in heaven—today. Friend, no matter what you're feeling today, here's what I want you to try with me:

- If you feel unseen, help one person feel seen by reminding her how uniquely beautiful and gifted she is today.
- If you feel unheard, help one person feel heard by holding space to listen when she's speaking to you and prayerfully ask God how you can encourage her.
- If you feel unnoticed, help one person feel noticed by honoring the amazing little things she does every single day to make the world a better place.

And why do all of this? Because I've found as we purposefully ease the ache in others, we will see it is beautifully eased in us.

The unseen ache. The unheard ache. The unnoticed ache.

Let's start with the people right in front of us today. And watch and see how God turns small into something big and beautiful in His timing.

As we purposefully ease the ache in others, we will see it is beautifully eased in us.

EVENING

Before this day ends, let's make some decisions together.

We want to live in a better world, right? So, let's make it better. Let's vow to bring heaven to earth with the loving words we say and the moments we cultivate that bring laughter.

It doesn't have to be big to be significant. We can show up, listen, and learn. We can pray and dream. We don't have to push or prove or earn anything.

We can plan something joyful.

We can plan for some moments that matter.

We can plan to do something for another person that will simply be kind and honor God.

I can't wait to see what beauty emerges tomorrow because we started looking for it today. Sweet dreams, sis. I love you. I thank God for you, and I believe in you.

SOMETHING TO RELEASE BACK TO GOD FROM TODAY:

_____

_____

A PRAYER TO RECEIVE BEFORE TOMORROW:

God, thank You for the ways You love me. I see Your faithfulness in big and small ways every single day. I pray You would show me small ways I can invest big-time into eternity by helping others You put in my path. Show me someone to encourage, someone to serve, someone who needs to be reminded that You are for her. I know I can't help everyone, but that doesn't mean I shouldn't help someone. In Jesus' name, amen.

14

A Good Friday Reminder
for an Ordinary Day

> "My soul is overwhelmed with sorrow to the point of death,"
> he said to them. "Stay here and keep watch."
>
> MARK 14:34

MORNING

We all know what it's like to wrestle through those deep disappointments in life that linger on and on. We've all had situations in which we've prayed countless prayers, pleading with God to intervene and make things different. Even Jesus lifted up tear-filled prayers of desperation for God to make things different.

Look at the words from this prayer Jesus prayed after He left the Last Supper with His disciples: "'My soul is overwhelmed with sorrow to the point of death,' he said to them. 'Stay here and keep watch'" (Mark 14:34).

In Mark 14, Jesus was in the garden of Gethsemane feeling the crushing weight of what He knew He must endure. He very much knew what He would soon experience during the crucifixion. Jesus knew that crushing-heart feeling. He felt it. He wrestled with it. He carried it.

I have found such comfort in remembering the humanity of Jesus in this scene in the garden of Gethsemane. Yes, Jesus was sinless, but He very much knew the overwhelming blows of being sinned against. Jesus understood betrayal, abuse, and being abandoned by people He should have been able to trust.

As you walk into this day, live encouraged that you're not walking alone in your pain. You're not walking misunderstood. You're walking with Jesus. He hears you. He sees you. He understands you.

A statement to remember as I walk into today:

Jesus was sinless, but He very much knew the overwhelming blows of being sinned against.

EVENING

Good Friday wasn't the end of the story for Jesus. And today doesn't have the final say in our stories either.

We got to read Mark 14 this morning knowing how the story ends. Good Friday is our reminder that when everything feels lost, when darkness seems to take over, there is hope on the way. We know a better ending because we know a victorious Savior. Darkness may last for a while, but joy comes in the morning (Psalm 30:5).

Oh friend, take heart. Keep holding on to the hope you have in Jesus. He really does understand the depth of carrying sorrow and hope at the same time.

Easter isn't just an annual celebration. It's a personal revelation for right now. It's where the unknowns of today feel less excruciating because of the certain victory of tomorrow.

Rest easily tonight knowing that Jesus is victorious and hope is on the way.

SOMETHING TO RELEASE BACK TO GOD FROM TODAY:

_____

_____

A PRAYER TO RECEIVE BEFORE TOMORROW:

Lord, thank You for the truths I've been reminded of today from Good Friday. Thank You for raising Jesus from the dead so we would forever have a tangible reminder of hope and a pathway to relationship with You. Give me the courage and strength to continue pressing in when things get hard. Remind me of Good Friday when I get discouraged. There is always hope for this moment and joy for tomorrow. In Jesus' name, amen.

15

You Can Love
Them, but You
Can't Change
Them

> Let us then approach God's throne of grace with confidence, so that we
> may receive mercy and find grace to help us in our time of need.
>
> HEBREWS 4:16

MORNING

Relationships are wonderful . . . until they're not.

All relationships can be difficult at times, but they should not be destructive to our well-being. If you have relationships in your life where you know something is wrong, but you can't for the life of you figure out what to do, I understand. I know what it feels like to have your body tense and your pulse quicken while your mind is begging the other person, *Stop doing this!*

Most of us aren't equipped to know what to do when we know things need to change but the other person isn't willing to or capable of cooperating with the needed changes. Your challenge may be with

- someone who personalizes everything and is prone to being offended, so you can't figure out how to address something this person repeatedly does that is not acceptable to you. You know you need a boundary, but you don't know how to communicate this need.
- a person in authority over you, and boundaries don't feel like they would work.
- a family member who lives in your home, and though you need some distance, setting a boundary doesn't feel realistic.

You've prayed about this behavior or situation. You've tried to navigate it. You've made changes. You may have even tried to stop it. You've listened to wise advice and done everything you know to do. But in the end, nothing has worked.

You've finally realized if they don't want things to change, you cannot change them. This is a terribly hard truth to accept, but it's one of the most freeing truths I've learned to embrace.

The only other option is secretly wondering if you are the crazy one. Friend, you may be brokenhearted. You may be sad. You may be afraid and possibly angry. You may be focused on trying to fix what isn't within your ability to fix. And you may even be fixated on trying to figure everything out.

But you are not crazy. If you are smelling smoke, there is fire. And the only reasonable option at this point is either to put out the fire or get yourself away from the fire. Drawing boundaries can help put out fires before they become all-consuming. But if the fire keeps burning with increasing intensity, you've got to get away from the smoke and flames. Sometimes your only option may be to distance yourself from this person and say goodbye.

Boundaries aren't going to fix the other person. But boundaries will help you stay fixed on what is good, what is acceptable, and what you need to stay healthy and whole.

I don't know what boundaries you may need to consider; I challenge you to process this situation with the Lord and prayerfully think through what changes may be necessary alongside a trusted Christian counselor or wise friend. Maybe for today, it's just enough to sit and think through the truth that the only sustainable change you have control over is making a sustainable change for yourself.

I know this isn't easy, but it is good.

Boundaries will help you stay fixed on what is good, what is acceptable, and what you need to stay healthy and whole.

EVENING

Even though we may be powerless to change someone else, this doesn't mean we're powerless to experience change in our own lives. Boundaries give us this gift.

Now that you've had some time to process the truth we talked about this morning, I want us to close our day considering some questions that could help us implement some necessary boundaries in our lives:

- What events or conversations have occurred that make you feel as if it's not acceptable to put relational parameters in place in this relationship?
- Are there certain behaviors this person exhibits that makes setting boundaries with him or her seem unrealistic or impossible?
- What good might be possible in this relationship if you set boundaries?
- What is and is not acceptable behavior?
- What are your deal breakers that would pull you from a place of health into unhealth?

- What are you actually responsible for? What are you not responsible for? (Example: "I am responsible for showing up to my job on time." "I am not responsible for my coworker's harsh reaction or response in a conversation.")
- What are some of the qualities you like about yourself that you want to make sure the people you love experience when they spend time with you? How can boundaries help make your best qualities more and more apparent?

Remember, friend, if someone is unwilling or unable to stop misusing the personal access we've given them in our lives, then we must create healthy boundaries.

After you've had time to consider these questions, tomorrow morning I'll give you five factors to help you set good boundaries. But for now, sweet dreams, friend.

SOMETHING TO RELEASE BACK TO GOD FROM TODAY:

_____

_____

A PRAYER TO RECEIVE BEFORE TOMORROW:

Lord, it's a humbling truth to realize I can't change another person; I can only change myself. As I process these questions and consider where setting healthy boundaries may be necessary, give me discernment, wisdom, and courage. In Jesus' name, amen.

DAY

16

Better
Boundaries
Lead to Better
Relationships

> Let your conversation be always full of grace, seasoned with salt, so that you may know how to answer everyone.
>
> COLOSSIANS 4:6

MORNING

Good morning, friend. I want to continue making progress concerning boundaries in our relationships today. As a refresher, go back and look at the questions listed in last night's devotion.

I want to give you five factors to help you set good boundaries in your everyday life. But before you read these, I want to encourage you in one thing: don't get overwhelmed as you read through all five of these things to remember. Setting boundaries in a healthy, God-honoring way most likely won't happen overnight. It's okay if you need some time to sit and process and pray over how setting healthy boundaries could improve your relationships and your personal life.

1. Remember, a boundary isn't to take control of the other person's actions.

The purpose of a boundary is to help you stay self-controlled and safe. A friend of mine recently said, "I thought I was setting a boundary, but I was actually just trying to control the situation by forcing the other person to change." If your focus is trying to change the other person, then you will quickly feel like boundaries don't work for you. It's time to shift your focus to what you can control with your boundary:

- your environment
- what you are, and are not, willing to tolerate
- what you do, and do not, have to give

Your boundary should help set the stage so your emotions can stay more regulated, you can regain a sense of safety, and you can feel empowered to make necessary changes.

2. Remember, grace has a place in this conversation.

We can be gracious in how we talk about our concerns, our need for a boundary, and the consequences if the boundary is violated. My counselor, Jim Cress, always says, "Say what you mean, mean what you say, and don't say it mean." Remember, a boundary will most likely mean a change in this relationship for you and for the other person. It's not wrong for them to ask questions and maybe even want to know a timeframe for how long this boundary will last. We can be gracious in how we inform the other person and answer any questions that are reasonable and appropriate.

Another helpful statement Jim taught me when having a potentially challenging conversation is, "Get curious, not furious." You may find it helpful to ask questions about the other person's concerns instead of making assumptions and accusations. Again, we don't want to overexplain or debate our need for this boundary. But we can be gracious in our communication around this boundary. Pre-decide and possibly even script out what you will say.

As a rule of thumb, I try to start with empathy and acknowledge something positive about the other person before addressing what I think must change. There are many Bible verses that could be helpful here, but one of my favorite verses I repeat to my frustrated self so often I have it memorized. Colossians 4:6 says, "Let your conversation be always full of grace, seasoned with salt, so that you may know how to answer everyone."

This doesn't mean we don't say the hard things or set boundaries. It means we recognize we want conflict resolution instead of conflict escalation.

3. Remember, boundaries help you fight for the relationship.

Boundaries are both for your sake and the other person's, so you don't have to keep fighting against unhealthy behaviors, attitudes, and patterns. We can either set a boundary, or we will set the stage for simmering resentments. Simmering in the frustrations of knowing things need to change, or trying to get the other person to change, is much more damaging than a boundaries conversation. Yes, boundaries can feel risky. But it's a much bigger risk to delay or refuse to have needed conversations.

4. Remember, a boundary without a real consequence will never be taken seriously.

We have to consider the consequences for crossed boundaries with wisdom and logic. A boundary presented as a hopeful wish is nothing but a weak suggestion. And a boundary presented as a threat will only do more damage. If we can't or won't follow through with a consequence, then that person will eventually stop respecting what we have to say and ignore all future boundary attempts. I've found it very helpful to think through consequences ahead of time and process them with my counselor or wise friends.

When you establish a boundary, it's in support of the relationship, not against it. This isn't an accusation against the other person. You are simply readjusting their access to match the level of responsibility they've demonstrated in the relationship. Unfortunately, it's often people who

need boundaries the most who will respect them the least. So don't be surprised or caught off guard if this happens. You can return kindness for this frustration and even empathy for their anger. But see this as affirmation that you are doing the right thing. Stand firm and state the consequences with dignity and respect.

5. Remember to play out how this boundary will benefit you.

Sometimes we feel the pain of setting a boundary, and that can make us forget the good reasons we're setting boundaries. In number three above, we talked about how boundaries are beneficial for both parties in the relationship. So, let's remember that there is also the benefit of what a boundary will do for us personally. We are taking responsibility to keep our own sanity, safety, and serenity in check. Like we learned yesterday, we aren't responsible for the other person's choices, but we are responsible for our actions and our reactions.

Remember, you set boundaries to help you stop feeling so stuck and powerless and allow yourself to get to a healthier place. It's important that you think through the positives of setting boundaries and rehearse stating them clearly beforehand from a place of strength, so if things get tough and emotional you won't give up. It will be challenging if you have to implement the consequences, but if you've already made peace with this process, you won't get nearly as confused and frustrated. Getting to a better place is good even if it doesn't feel good in the moment.

A statement to remember as I walk into today:

Getting to a better place is good even if it doesn't feel good in the moment.

EVENING

Friend, I know how challenging it can be to accept the truth that we can't change others. I know how it feels to look at chaos around you and think, *How can I possibly not try to take control of the situation?*

But here's what I know: we shouldn't work harder on that person than they're willing to work on themselves. Even if you get a person off the tracks at this moment, they will climb right back on them tomorrow. If your heart is more committed to change than the other person's is, then you may delay the train wreck, but you will not be able to save them from it. And from what I've experienced, the more you keep jumping onto the tracks to try and rescue someone, the more likely it is that the train will run over you both.

I don't say that lightly. I say it lovingly because it's true. I wish with every fiber of my being I could tell you that you can do enough to one day cause that person to change . . . to give enough . . . to love enough . . . to forgive enough . . . to beg enough . . . to talk enough . . . or to control enough. But it's not true. Change can only happen for them from the inside out. Truly sustainable, lasting change must come from inside the person's own heart, not from pressure exerted from the outside.

Now, this doesn't mean that we don't continue to care about this person. Nor does it mean that we cut them out entirely, forever. But it does mean we change our role and job description. We want them saved, but we are not their Savior.

Before this day ends, open your hands and release the efforts you've been tirelessly pouring out to someone, hoping things will finally take a turn for the better. I'm so sorry for what you're facing in this relationship. I know how hard it is on your heart. But I have seen healthy boundaries really help in my own life, and I want the same for you.

Maybe this is your next step toward healing. I know you're going to make it, friend. Good night.

SOMETHING TO RELEASE BACK TO GOD FROM TODAY:

_____

_____

A PRAYER TO RECEIVE BEFORE TOMORROW:

God, thank You for the truths in Your Word that help us walk through situations in our everyday lives. As I navigate different relationship struggles, I know You will show me how to love others well without losing the best of who I am in the process. I love You, Lord. In Jesus' name, amen.

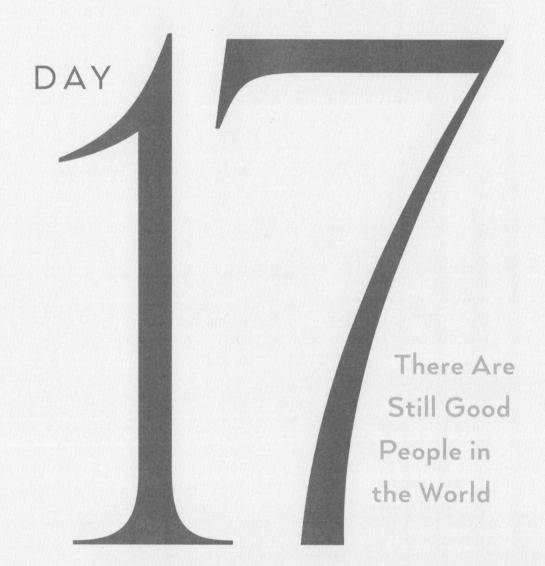

DAY

17

There Are
Still Good
People in
the World

> Who may ascend the mountain of the LORD?
> Who may stand in his holy place? The one
> who has clean hands and a pure heart.
>
> PSALM 24:3-4

MORNING

When life gets hard, we may feel justified if our hearts also get hard and the lens through which we see the world becomes tainted by past hurts.

When this happens, we stop believing the best can still happen in our circumstances. We stop believing the best about people. We carry the wrong that one person did to us into other relationships and become overly guarded and overly suspicious that history will repeat itself. We can easily start assuming this other person will hurt us, too, and we start assigning to them wrong intentions they don't have.

But friend, if we were sitting together over coffee today, I would reach for your hand and encourage you with this: when life gets hard, let your heart stay soft. Let your thoughts stay true.

Don't fill in the gaps with worst-case scenarios. Don't assume what others are thinking. You can listen to your discernment. If something feels off or untrue, ask questions, verify answers, and realize sometimes people aren't honest. But at the same time, remember there are many other people who are honest, true, and real.

The world is full of good-hearted people. People who want the best for you. People who cling to the truth of God's Word and encourage you with the wisdom-filled words from it. Do life with those people. Embrace the gift of those people.

Even though life may look different than you thought it would, it can still be stunningly beautiful. Make the choice right here and right now that you're going to let your heart stay soft and believe there's still goodness to be found today.

A statement to remember as I walk into today:

When life gets hard, let your heart stay soft.

EVENING

Today, I was reminded there are some amazing people in this world.

The ones who live the gospel message in the most real and beautiful ways. The ones who don't make much of what they do. They just honor God. I'm so grateful for them.

Take a moment to thank God for some of the people in your life who showed you much of Jesus today. Send a quick text before you go to sleep to let them know how much they mean to you.

As we thank God for these friends in our lives, let's also pray that we would become more and more like this kind of friend too.

SOMETHING TO RELEASE BACK TO GOD FROM TODAY:

_____

_____

A PRAYER TO RECEIVE BEFORE TOMORROW:

Dear Lord, thank You for the gift of friendship I have with the women I get to do life with. I pray today that You would show me how to uplift, encourage, and meet a need for those in my community. Put someone on my heart today who needs a touch of love and encouragement. In Jesus' name, amen.

DAY

18

When You're Tempted to Judge Her

Let your gentleness be evident to all.

PHILIPPIANS 4:5

MORNING

Almost every day, I talk to people who are hurting for many different reasons.

When we're in the middle of hurting, one of the hardest parts isn't just the situation we're dealing with but also the compounded hurt from others doing things that unknowingly add to our pain.

Assumptions made.
Blame assigned.
Labels given.
Judgment cast.

Whether we know someone is hurting or not, we can make a decision this morning: *we will be people of gentleness.*

Your coworker? Your friend? The woman at Bible study who never seems to engage? That stranger whose child was screaming in the grocery store? The neighbor who always seems grumpy and complains about everyone on your street? Maybe she's processing some kind of pain you don't know about. Or she's trying to figure out something very complicated. Chances are that she is facing or has faced something challenging. How do I know that? Because she is a human living in the same confusing, often chaotic, and hard-to-understand world that often breaks your heart and mine.

We don't have to know all the details of her story. But we can be gentle when we cross paths with her.

Instead of our first reaction being to label her based on what she is *doing* right now, let's pray for her based on what she's probably *facing* right now. And if possible, why not offer a rare voice of encouragement or an unexpected act of kindness?

We may not be able to help the whole world be a better place today. But why not help the ones God places right in front of us? Judgment can end with us when gentleness flows through us. Together, let's show her a little less judgment and a lot more of Jesus today.

A statement to remember as I walk into today: —————— | | | | | | | ———

Judgment can end with us when gentleness flows from us.

EVENING

There was a time in my life when my heart hurt so deeply, not much helped.

But I remember one ordinary day when one of my friends randomly dropped off dinner for me. She didn't even ask to come inside. She just texted me that she left dinner on the front porch, allowing me to have my space while making sure I knew she was there for me.

I cried because I had just prayed for God to help me. And then my friend showed up.

Even though the soup she made wasn't the solution for what I was facing, I felt a lot less alone. And I felt seen by God.

Before the end of this day, let's pray that we will be more aware of the people all around us who are hurting. You can love and help and pray for someone without knowing the full story. Help with an obvious small need. Pray for what you *do* know.

And when we suddenly find ourselves in the seat of suffering (and all of us will be there at some point), what we've modeled to others will often be returned back to us. So tonight, let's release to God both our hesitancies to help others and our resistance to receive help from others.

SOMETHING TO RELEASE BACK TO GOD FROM TODAY:

_____

_____

A PRAYER TO RECEIVE BEFORE TOMORROW:

God, I pray for that person who came to my mind as I was reading today's devotion. I pray for Your comfort and peace to be her closest companion right now. I pray You would encourage the hurting places of her heart. Help her confidently believe You are still working on her behalf even when she can't see it. When I'm tempted to make assumptions or cast judgment in any way, help me put on gentleness so she can see more of You through me. And remind me to do something kind for her. I may not know what she needs, but You do. Help me know too. In Jesus' name, amen.

DAY

19

Laying
Down
What
Was Never
Mine to Carry

> Come to me, all you who are weary and
> burdened, and I will give you rest.
>
> MATTHEW 11:28

MORNING

I've been carrying a burden that's been weighing me down for a long time.

And today, right now, this minute, I'm choosing to lay it down. I'm releasing it to God. And I'm making a commitment to not pick it back up.

I suspect you might have a similar situation in which you keep trying to control something or someone completely out of your control.

- It's that situation you can't fix, but you keep fretting about it anyhow.
- It's that desire to change a person who isn't willing to change, but you keep working harder on them than they are willing to work on themselves.
- It's that expectation you know is unrealistic, but you keep letting your disappointment hijack your emotions.
- It's that longing you say you've given to God, but you keep working behind the scenes, desperate to arrange it yourself.

We can be responsible to do what we should do in all of these scenarios. But we shouldn't try to do what only God can do. Today is a great day to say, "Enough. I've done my part, and now I must let God do His part."

We can make the choice to lay down burdens that were never ours to carry.

Together, let's be obedient to God by declaring we will trust Him with what we are laying down. Then let's fill that time we were spending carrying this burden with other life-giving pursuits. And let's resolve to leave the rest up to Him.

A statement to remember as I walk into today:

We shouldn't try to do what only God can do.

EVENING

Sometimes I think I hold tightly to burdens I need to release because I don't see tangible evidence of God doing anything.

I see no change. No intervention. No breakthrough. But this is what I'm reminding myself of as I attempt to lay down what isn't mine to carry: *we don't serve a do-nothing God.*

God is working. Even in the silence and the unknown.

That means I can stop pushing. I can stop trying to control. I can stop trying to make people something they aren't. I can embrace the truth that there is a Savior of the world, but it isn't me. This doesn't mean I give up. It means I'm giving over to God what was never mine to carry.

Release that burden you've decided to return back to God. And then get some rest. God's got this.

SOMETHING TO RELEASE BACK TO GOD FROM TODAY:

_____

_____

A PRAYER TO RECEIVE BEFORE TOMORROW:

God, as I rest tonight, I'm asking for Your help as I release this burden that feels really heavy. I'm trusting You with it all—the outcomes, the questions, the unknowns. Help me remember that even if I tried to keep carrying this, I wouldn't be able to control the outcome. You're the perfect, sufficient Savior who already knows the future, who isn't caught off guard by any of it, and who knows how to lead me through it. The more I trust You with this, the less I will suffer trying to carry it all myself. I love You. In Jesus' name, amen.

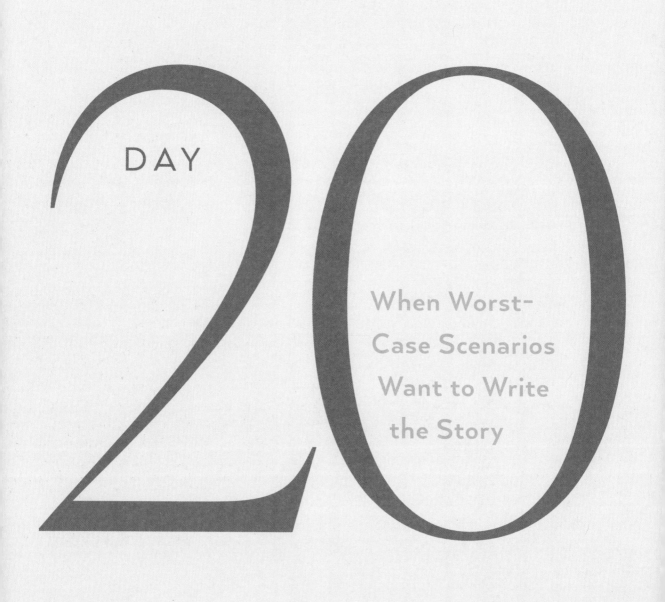

DAY

20

When Worst-
Case Scenarios
Want to Write
the Story

Do not be anxious about anything, but in every situation, by prayer and petition, with thanksgiving, present your requests to God. And the peace of God, which transcends all understanding, will guard your hearts and your minds in Christ Jesus.

PHILIPPIANS 4:6-7

MORNING

There's something I've learned about myself recently: sometimes what's really overwhelming me isn't that I have too much to do or too much to process; it's that I've allowed too much fear into the mix of it all.

Fear of the unknown.
Fear of what crazy thing is going to hit next.
Fear of not being able to see when or if "normal" will ever return.

Can you relate?

Sometimes what is really causing me to be afraid isn't what's actually in front of me—it's me projecting all the fearful possibilities onto what I'm facing today. I have a habit of mentally running into the future, painting pictures of all the worst-case scenarios, and then running back to today and pinning those pictures all over the walls in my mind.

But as God is my witness, no worst-case-scenario thinking has ever protected me. It's only projected the possible pain of tomorrow into my day today and fed more fear.

Today, I'm asking God to help me know the difference between wise discernment and fear. And there is a big difference: One prompts me to remember God. The other prompts me to panic. And we can't live in panic and at peace at the same time.

Instead of trying to figure out the future and risk panicking because of worst-case scenarios, I intentionally look back at all the places in my life where I can clearly see that God had a good plan—He provided for me, He came through for me, and He helped me through whatever I faced. Tracing God's hand of faithfulness from our pasts is so much more calming than trying to predict the future. Let's lay down our worst-case-scenario stories and see how differently we feel and how differently we pray.

We can't live in panic and at peace at the same time.

EVENING

One thing that has helped me when I'm crippled with fear and don't understand what's in front of me is to whisper this prayer: "God, help me. Be with me. Lead me. Hold me. Show me the next step."

Often my next step isn't walking forward; it's gaining the assurance of God's faithfulness by remembering who He is. We already worked this morning on tracing His hand of faithfulness by looking at how He helped us in the past. Now, before we go to bed tonight, let's park our minds on who God is. And let's remember, God will never act inconsistently with who He is.

God is loving. God is kind. God is patient. God is just. God is all-capable and all-knowing. God is forgiving. God is generous. God is good.

Pray those truths about who God is, and feel His comfort tonight.

Then take a moment and glance outside. Look into that big expanse of stars and acknowledge that today the sky didn't fall. We don't have to fear. We don't have to worry about what's ahead. The same God who kept all the galaxies in place today will be right there to greet us and lead us into the daylight tomorrow.

SOMETHING TO RELEASE BACK TO GOD FROM TODAY:

_____

_____

A PRAYER TO RECEIVE BEFORE TOMORROW:

Father God, when I'm tempted to let worst-case scenarios write and rewrite the truth I believe, remind me You are in control. Remind me You can be trusted with it all. Remind me I don't have to run ahead and be prepared for it all because You hold it all together. Infuse my heart with hope and help me infuse hope into others too. In Jesus' name, amen.

DAY

21

Reclaiming
the Truth of
Who We Are

> **And so we know and rely on the love God has for us. God is love.
> Whoever lives in love lives in God, and God in them.**
>
> 1 JOHN 4:16

MORNING

A couple of years ago, my team at Proverbs 31 Ministries was brainstorming a new T-shirt concept.

Once it was designed, printed, and delivered, it was time to photograph the T-shirt for the bookstore. And I volunteered.

Now, here's something you need to know about me. I'm not usually the one who raises her hand and says, "I'll volunteer to model that shirt!" Nope. Modeling is not my thing.

But this shirt had words on it that felt so personal to me: *known and loved.*

Known and loved had been an anthem drumming in the background during some really hard days when I wondered if I'd survive the circumstances I was facing. And I knew taking a picture of me wearing this truth would be a good way to declare what I desperately wanted to feel.

Because instead of feeling known and loved, I felt forgotten and tossed aside. I needed a reminder to turn to God, open up His Word, and listen to praise songs. When I did those things, I could hear the anthem of God's voice rising above the chaos: *Lysa, you are known and so very loved by Me. Trust Me. Turn to Me. Hold on to Me.* He held me when I could barely hang on, and He reminded me what was true of me when I was tempted to forget.

I survived. And so will you.

I pray those two words—*known* and *loved*—remind you of what God wants you to know today. Even if you don't feel loved. Even if you don't feel known or understood. Remember, our feelings aren't always an accurate assessment of what's true. Cling to the words of our verse today: "And so we know and rely on the love God has for us. God is love. Whoever lives in love lives in God, and God in them" (1 John 4:16).

A statement to remember as I walk into today:

Today and every day: God knows you, and God loves you.

EVENING

Sweet friend, I don't know who in your life has told you that you are anything less than the most glorious creation of the almighty God. I don't know who has spoken words over you and about you that have stripped you bare and broken your heart.

But I do know whatever statement was spoken to you that came against the truth must be called a lie. God's Word is the truth. And His truth says you are a holy and dearly loved child of your heavenly Father.

You are wonderfully made.
You are a treasure.
You are beautiful.
You are fully known by Him and lavishly loved by Him.
You are chosen.
You are special.
You are set apart.

Tonight, release a lie you've been believing that makes you feel less than who you are. Then set your mind and heart on these things and remember God's words. Repeat God's words. Believe God's words with your whole heart.

SOMETHING TO RELEASE BACK TO GOD FROM TODAY:

_____

_____

A PRAYER TO RECEIVE BEFORE TOMORROW:

Jesus, thank You for the truth-filled words of Scripture that are always there to remind me who I really am. When my own insecurities rise up or hurtful comments from others threaten to disrupt this truth, help me believe I am known and loved. Cared for and prayed for. Chosen and cherished. In Jesus' name, amen.

DAY

22

Don't Stop
Praying;
Don't Stop
Crying Out

*Rejoice always, pray continually, give thanks in all circumstances;
for this is God's will for you in Christ Jesus.*

1 THESSALONIANS 5:16–18

MORNING

Is there a prayer you've been waiting on God to answer for so long that you're just about ready to give up?

I understand that in a deeply personal way.

We know God can do anything, but we can't understand why He doesn't seem to intervene for us right now. I get it, and I've cried many tears because of it.

It's hard when we are living in that space where our head knows God could do anything, but our hearts are heavy because He's not doing what we are hoping for, what we've prayed for, and what we've believed for . . . for a long while.

My friend, before you throw in the towel, I want to encourage you this morning.

Keep pressing into God. Keep praying. Don't pull away. He isn't ignoring you; He is listening. He loves you too much to answer your prayers at any other time than the right time and in any other way than the right way.

I will be the one to bear witness to your pain today and say that whatever you are believing God for, I am believing for it *with you*. He hears you and sees you and is aware of the tears you've shed and the pain you're experiencing (Psalm 56:8–9). Sometimes, the miracle He offers us does not change our circumstances or bring us the answers we desperately want, but He promises to remain near to us and to continue working in us. And that is a divine miracle I'm so very thankful for.

Keep filling the space where your heart aches with prayer. He is on the move even if things don't look like what we thought they would right now. Keep crying out to Him.

Remember, sometimes the reason we feel God isn't answering us is because we keep expecting His answer to look exactly like our expectations. Since His thoughts are higher than ours and His ways better than ours, I have to believe His answers will be more in keeping with what's really best for us. That's why following Him is called *faith*. The sooner we trust Him with the outcomes, the more clearly we will be able to see evidence of His faithfulness and signs of the goodness He is weaving into our stories today.

A statement to remember as I walk into today:

God loves you too much to answer your prayers at any other time than the right time and in any other way than the right way.

EVENING

In case you climb into bed tonight feeling tired, short of words, and unsure what to pray, I want to share my favorite prayer with you. Read this over yourself:

God, I want to see You.
God, I want to hear You.
God, I want to follow hard after You.
And I know . . .
God, You are good.
You are good to me.
You are good at being God.
Therefore, I trade my will for Your will, because I'm assured that You will guide me through this.

Thank You that I don't have to figure everything out. As today ends, I want to declare what my mindset and actions will be for tomorrow: I'm intentionally going to look for someone to forgive and someone to bless as I notice the evidence all around me of Your goodness and faithfulness.

Tonight, release an expectation you've been clinging to for what you think a good God should do.

God is writing a beautiful story for you, friend. You can rest peacefully and wake up encouraged knowing God is doing more on your behalf behind the scenes than you could ever imagine.

SOMETHING TO RELEASE BACK TO GOD FROM TODAY:

_____

_____

A PRAYER TO RECEIVE BEFORE TOMORROW:

Heavenly Father, thank You for always hearing my prayers. Help me not grow weary in my prayer life but instead use it to grow my faith in Your sure strength and capabilities. I trust You with all of my heart and all of the outcomes I'm praying for. In Jesus' name, amen.

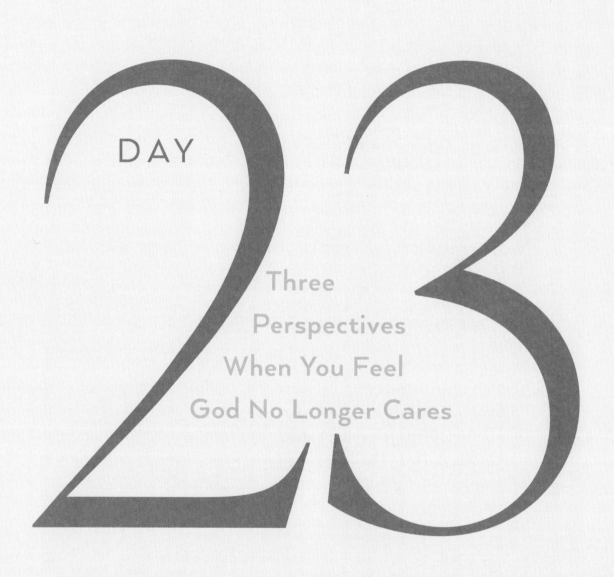

DAY

23

Three
Perspectives
When You Feel
God No Longer Cares

> The LORD is close to the brokenhearted and saves
> those who are crushed in spirit.
>
> PSALM 34:18

MORNING

God, are You there? Don't You see what I'm walking through? I thought as I looked in the mirror. I felt weary. And I was tired of hurting.

One of the hardest places to be emotionally is not when we're brokenhearted but when we begin to believe God no longer cares.

Oh, friend, I love you too much to let you believe that lie. God is here. God cares. No matter what circumstances you woke up to this morning, receive these three truths and let the words inform your heart of what is ultimately true:

1. *God often works in the unseen.* Just because we can't see it or feel it doesn't mean He's doing nothing. God isn't hiding from us; He's waiting to be seen by us. Let's be noticers today of what He is doing and what He is providing.
2. *God often speaks quietly to our hearts.* Is there something God has been prompting you to do that you've been resisting or delaying? Ask for the grace and courage to take that step today. The one who obeys God's instruction today will be able to discern His direction more clearly tomorrow.
3. *Don't mistake what feels like a lack of intervention as a sign of His lack of affection.* Look for ways God is showing you assurances of His love. His deep affection is all around you today.

Today isn't the whole story, friend. Not even close.

A statement to remember as I walk into today:

God isn't hiding from us; He's waiting to be seen by us.

EVENING

When we're hurting, it's easy to believe we'll always feel like this. That life will always be this hard.

But every now and then, we catch glimpses of beauty that feel so right. Little reminders to our souls that God is real and good and heaven is closer than we think.

I wonder if these moments are like arrows pointing us home to heaven. When those moments come, let yourself linger in that beautiful space you discover. Soak it up and store up every bit of courage you can from those moments.

I believe God puts beauty in front of us as a reminder that He is the creator of good. And He is working good for you as well.

This is what I know: your one incredible, brilliant, beautiful life should never be reduced to the limitations of living hurt. There's a great big world out there. There are new adventures and amazing possibilities you don't want to miss. So grow into God's grace, giving it kindly and accepting it freely.

It's time to get moving and get on with living. This is the beauty of trusting God in the midst of our healing. Sweet dreams, friend.

SOMETHING TO RELEASE BACK TO GOD FROM TODAY:

_____

_____

A PRAYER TO RECEIVE BEFORE TOMORROW:

God, even when I feel hurt, help me not to live hurt. Remind me of what's true in the middle of what feels hard. Open my eyes to see what's still possible and beautiful and lovely and fun even when my heart is hurting. Thank You for never leaving me alone to figure it out all on my own. In Jesus' name, amen.

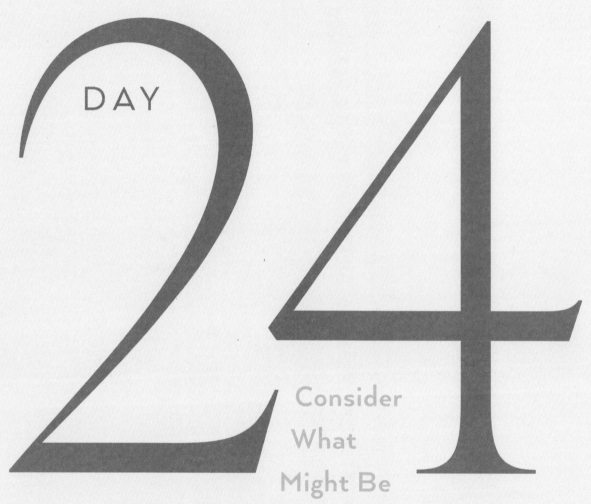

DAY

24

Consider
What
Might Be
Possible in the Middle of
What Feels Impossible

Jesus looked at them and said, "With man this is impossible,
but not with God; all things are possible with God."

MARK 10:27

MORNING

I've made peace with the fact that sorrow and celebration can coexist. In one single day together. One month together. One season together.

You don't have to pick one or the other. A person can quite simply have both.

If you're struggling to see possibility and potential in the middle of what feels hard, here's an incomplete but potentially beautiful recipe for making things better:

- Honesty.
- Refusal to be led by my unhealthy or insecure thoughts.
- Letting myself laugh today. Letting myself cry today. Letting myself enjoy trying something new. And letting myself sit with a memory of something I miss.
- Prayers for God to help me be true to my most healed, healthy, and holy mindset.
- Peace with the fact I will disappoint people. Peace with the fact other people will disappoint me. And the perspective that not every disappointment is epic.
- Permission to be human while choosing not to excuse or justify behaviors that hurt others.
- Grace to let others sometimes be fragile, fickle, and forgetful without my labeling them by their mistakes.
- Wisdom to know I can be both wise and whimsical. Steady and emotional. Mature and a mess in progress.
- Forgiveness for what can't be changed and willingness to talk about and act on what can be changed.

Not all of these may be possible for you today. But just consider . . . which one of these *could* be possible? What could be possible if you tried? You don't have to do it perfectly for it to be good. Remember, we must not let the sorrow of yesterday cloud the celebration of new possibilities for today.

We must not let the sorrow of yesterday cloud the celebration of new possibilities for today.

EVENING

I know it can be very challenging to find the energy to enjoy the people still in your life when someone you loved has left your life. It can be painful to imagine life feeling good and normal and hopeful again. It can feel like when this one part ended, everything else about life sort of ended as well.

But let me speak life into your worn-out, broken-down, hurting heart before you go to sleep: there's always a way with God. Even when things look impossible, there's always possibilities with God. There's always potential with God.

Stay close to Him. Stay close to people who love Him. Stay believing and looking for what's possible in the middle of what looks so impossible. See the word *impossible* as God reminding you, *I'm possible.* And rest in that as you go to sleep.

Tonight, release the belief that a dead end is the end to all you hoped life would look like, and open your heart to the hopeful possibilities for the future.

SOMETHING TO RELEASE BACK TO GOD FROM TODAY:

_____

_____

A PRAYER TO RECEIVE BEFORE TOMORROW:

Jesus, as I go to sleep tonight, I'm releasing all that feels impossible into Your hands. I pray Your peace would flood my mind and my heart and ease any uncertainty I'm feeling. Help me look to You in my circumstances and see Your goodness and faithfulness even here. Help me not to be so consumed with my sorrow that I miss the chance to celebrate what You are bringing into my life right now. In Jesus' name, amen.

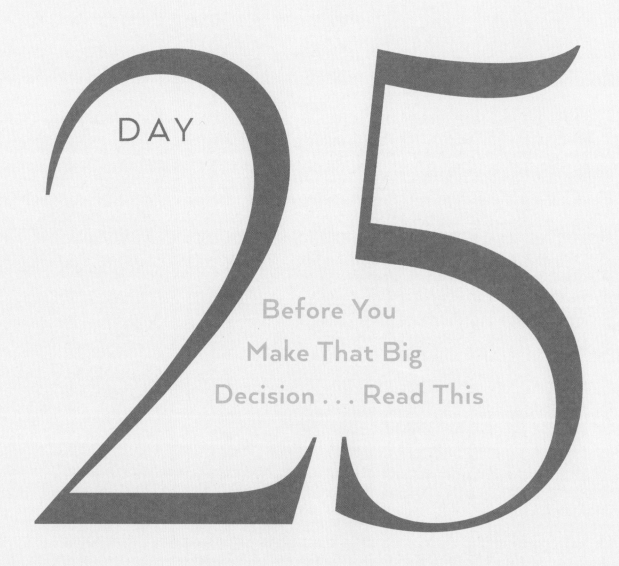

DAY

25

Before You
Make That Big
Decision . . . Read This

How can a young person stay on the path of purity?
By living according to your word.

PSALM 119:9

MORNING

Is there a decision you're wrestling through today?

Maybe you're considering a job change, a relationship boundary you need to set, or which events to say yes and no to this month? Even if it's not one of these things, chances are that there is some decision you're praying about, thinking about, or anticipating.

Here's what I know: The two most powerful words are *yes* and *no*. How we use those words not only communicates the decisions we make but also the intention of our hearts and the direction of our lives.

We don't want to overthink every decision we have to make, but we also don't want to underthink either. Here are a few questions to help you think through your decisions:

- Is it leading you closer to God's best or detouring away from it?
- Is it supported by the wisdom of trusted friends who lean on God's Word and listen to God's leading?
- When you ask for other people's advice, are you withholding any necessary details, hoping they will agree with you rather than challenge you?
- When you think about this decision, do you feel more at peace or panicked?
- Is this a decision that feels good for today but could have negative consequences long term?
- What will this decision cost you, and is it a cost you're willing to pay?

My friend, I feel an urgent need to hold your hand and tenderly guide you toward godly wisdom. Sometimes the wise answer won't feel convenient. Sometimes the wise answer won't feel fair or fun. Sometimes the wise answer will require you to trust God patiently and not try to make something happen on your own. But if we want to live in the fruitfulness of being a wise person, we must choose wisdom over and over in our daily lives. Wisdom makes decisions today that are still good for tomorrow. That's what I want for myself. And that's what I want for you too.

We won't always get this right. And certainly in the past, we've all made choices we wish we wouldn't have. But let's remember that yesterday's decisions don't have to define today. Pre-decide this morning that no matter what choices seem attractive today, you will go with what most closely aligns with God's Word.

Wisdom makes decisions today that are still good for tomorrow.

EVENING

Recently, I surveyed people through my social media with this question: "What do you think is the biggest reason people struggle to make decisions?"

Overwhelmingly, the answer was *fear*.

Fear of the unknown.
Fear of getting hurt.
Fear of what others will think.
Fear of making the wrong decision.

I absolutely understand all these fears. I wrestle with them myself. And some wrestling with fear is good. But at times I still feel like I'm wrestling with fear to the point where I'm paralyzed from moving forward.

Here's an answer you must know when trying to make decisions: there is no choice that will turn out perfectly in every way.

As long as you desire to please God with your decisions, no decision you make will be completely awful. Nor will any decision you make be completely awesome. Every decision is a package deal of both good and challenging. In other words, since there is no perfect choice, I don't have to be paralyzed by the fear that I'm not making the *exact* right decision.

Remember this today, friend. We don't have to be perfect; we just need to be obedient.

God's promises are not dependent on our ability to choose well but rather on His ability to use well.

You can rest peacefully tonight knowing it's not about you getting every decision right. It's about staying close to God and letting Him lead you through it all. Sweet dreams, friend.

SOMETHING TO RELEASE BACK TO GOD FROM TODAY:

_____

_____

A PRAYER TO RECEIVE BEFORE TOMORROW:

Dear Lord, I trust You beyond any fear I have of making the wrong decision. Today, I hand over all my uncertainties to You. Steady my heart as I navigate decisions I have to make. Reveal Yourself to me. In Jesus' name, amen.

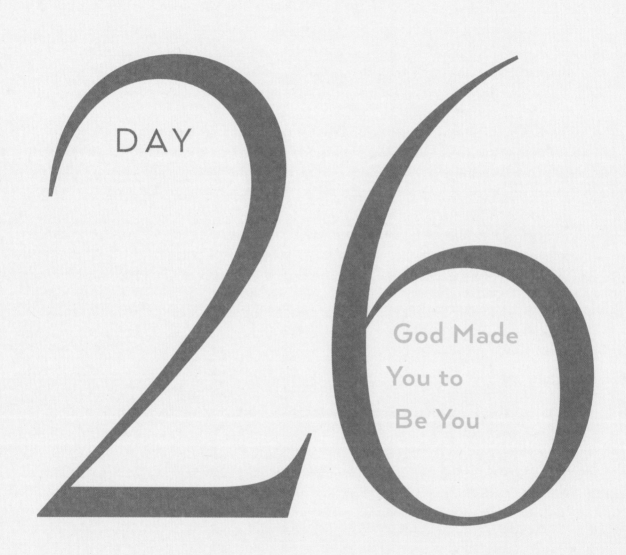

DAY

26

God Made
You to
Be You

For we are his workmanship, created in Christ Jesus for good works, which God prepared beforehand, that we should walk in them.

EPHESIANS 2:10 ESV

MORNING

A few years ago, a rush of nerves came over me right before I spoke to a large group of Christian counselors I respect so much. Hello, vulnerable. Hello, being afraid that they might analyze not just my message but my mental health as well.

As I was praying backstage, wishing I hadn't said yes to this opportunity and feeling afraid of this assignment before me, I asked God to help me. The other speakers were so impressive with their abilities to wow the crowd, and they beautifully fulfilled their assignment in being there. Some had impressive degrees, and others rallied the crowd to their feet with their bold declarations and high energy.

I didn't have any of that.

Just before I walked out, the Lord whispered into my heart: *Bring what you do have, and it will please Me.* I had empathy and a deep understanding of what it feels like when your life suddenly gets turned upside down and you have to learn to live that way for a while. None of that felt impressive. It felt so very ordinary. But the Lord was clear that those counselors didn't need a polished presentation by some perfectly put-together person. They needed a tender conversation. Reminders from His Word. Love. A friend to encourage them. A fellow human they could relate to and connect with.

As soon as I realized what the Lord really wanted from me in that moment, my fear started to lessen. I wasn't there to impress them; I was there to connect with them.

As I took the stage, I simply stated I didn't want them to think of me as a speaker and them as the audience. I wanted them to imagine we were old friends gathered because of a shared love for the Lord and a desire to learn how to do life better together through His Word. As I shared what I'd been walking through and some wisdom that could help them in their hard places, I felt calm and deeply connected to every person sitting in that room.

I've never forgotten that. It taught me something important: I am most brave when I am most aware of what the Lord wants from me. Then I can just settle in to be His best version of me.

I can inhale His approval of me.

I can exhale the fear, nerves, and pressure.

I can embrace the steady confidence of being exactly who He's made me to be.

I don't know what you're anxious about today, but I do know the Lord does not intend for you to feel the impossible pressure to be someone you're not. He isn't asking you to impress others. He's asking for you to connect with others. Remember, what's impressive to others often intimidates them. What's real and helpful to others often inspires them.

Before this day takes off, breathe in His promises for you. Shake off the anxiety. And fulfill God's assignments to help others in the way He's wired you with assurance.

God isn't asking you to impress others. He's asking for you to connect with others.

EVENING

What opportunity has the fear of failure been stealing from you lately?

I know how compelling fear can sound in your mind sometimes.

But friend, lean in and receive these words: Failure isn't the worst thing that can happen. Refusing God's invitation is far worse.

Achievement isn't always God's goal for us. He wants us to learn perseverance and courage and humility. So even failure has its gifts. Whether you succeed or not, as long as you are surrendered to Him, God can bring good from it all.

Refuse to stay stuck in a prison of fear, and dare to walk in obedience to God's whispered instruction. Break away from fear and embrace the possibilities of hope.

Hope comes alive when we decide to step out and find out what God made us to be and do.

SOMETHING TO RELEASE BACK TO GOD FROM TODAY:

_____

_____

God, I can't listen to Your leading when I'm feeling intimidated by others or when I'm trying to impress others. Help me silence those defeating scripts that my fears and insecurities are fueling. Keep my eyes, ears, and heart open to what You ask of me. I love You. In Jesus' name, amen.

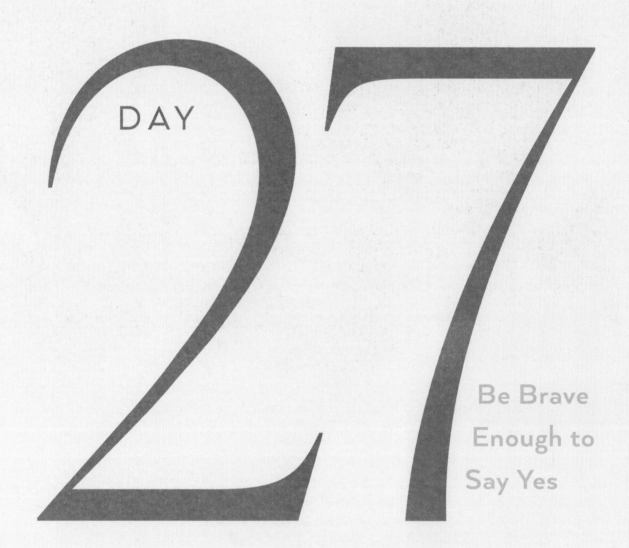

DAY

27

Be Brave
Enough to
Say Yes

Then I heard the voice of the Lord saying, "Whom shall I send?
And who will go for us?" And I said, "Here am I. Send me!"

ISAIAH 6:8

MORNING

Wherever you are this morning, God has you on assignment.

Big or small—it is very significant to Him. That's why breaking away from fear is so important. It frees us to say yes to God and walk through the doors He opens for us.

God might take you on unlikely paths through quiet seasons where you wonder if you heard Him wrong. You'll feel unnoticed. You'll wrestle with doubt. And in the harder moments, you might even question God: *Why do other people's assignments feel more fast-tracked than mine?*

I've been there.

But here's what almost thirty years in ministry has taught me: it's crucial to trust God in the small places. He will meet you there and prepare you there. God's preparing of you in the smaller assignments will be the saving of you in the bigger assignments.

And it's not even really about the assignment at all; it's about staying in alignment with His heart.

When Jesus is leading you somewhere that doesn't quite seem to line up with your expectations, remember His words, "Come, follow me" (Matthew 4:19), and then go. Say yes.

Where is Jesus inviting you to follow Him today, friend? What might be possible if you say yes?

A woman who stays close to Jesus and honors Him with each step she takes, both big and small—she changes the world! Say yes to being that kind of woman today.

A statement to remember as I walk into today:

God's preparing of you in the smaller assignments will be the saving of you in the bigger assignments.

EVENING

Be brave.

Friend, you know why you're reading this. You just needed to see it in writing. So, tonight, this one's for you:

You're stronger than you know.

You're held safe in our great God's mercy. He will be with you.

Don't get terrified or dismayed because of the stuff you don't understand or the things ahead that look scary.

Even if you can't see the whole pathway forward, trust that goodness is ahead. Cling to His truth, and let God light the way step-by-step.

Resolve in your soul that wherever God is leading is wherever you want to be.

Don't forget this tonight, sweet friend. Be brave.

SOMETHING TO RELEASE BACK TO GOD FROM TODAY:

_____

_____

A PRAYER TO RECEIVE BEFORE TOMORROW:

Father God, thank You for helping me choose to trust You wherever You lead me. I may not always feel brave, but I want to do what pleases You. Help me do that. Help me walk in the significant assignments You have given me—small, big, and every size in between. In Jesus' name, amen.

DAY

28

Even When Our Circumstances
Fall Apart, We Don't Have To

MORNING

I don't know what hard reality is crushing your heart this morning.

But here's what I do know: the Enemy is on a full-out attack against everything good, sacred, pure, and honest. He is the father of lies (John 8:44), and he wants us to believe that if our circumstances fall apart, then so will we.

But Satan is a liar. And what he has to say just isn't true.

In the middle of our own hard realities, let's spend some time recalling what *is* true about God and therefore what is true about us:

- God loves us, and He will not leave us. Even if we feel lonely, that doesn't mean we are alone.
- The battle we're facing right now belongs to the Lord. We can do our part. But then we must trust Him with the outcome. He will fight for us. We can save our emotional energy and use it to dig into His Word like never before. Even if we feel like we have to fix our circumstances, a better strategy is to fix our hearts and focus our minds on the reality that God is working and everything God touches is eventually redeemed.
- This battle might not be easy or short-lived, but victory will be there for those who trust God. Even if what God is allowing today doesn't feel good, we can trust that He is good and what He leads us to, He will lead us through.
- God is good even when the circumstances are darker than we ever imagined. God is good even when people are not. God is good even when things seem hopeless. God is good at being God. Even when we can't see the way out, God sees the bigger picture. He knows the way, and He will reveal the way step-by-step if we stick with Him day by day.
- God is the Redeemer. The Healer. The Author of hope. The Pathway of restoration.

Sweet friend, be still and know that He is God (Psalm 46:10). Even when it feels like the world is against us, God is for us.

A statement to remember as I walk into today:

The battle I'm facing today belongs to the Lord.

EVENING

If your day was less than shiny and bright . . . keep reading.

Light fights—and wins. No matter how hard the darkness tries to shut it out, the brightness always breaks through. It only takes the smallest amount of light to defeat an overwhelming amount of darkness. Slivers of light find their way into dark spaces. And the thing that always amazes me is that light shines brightest when the environment around it is the darkest.

This is true with physical light. And it's true with spiritual light as well. Jesus defeated the darkness of sin and hopelessness. He did it for me. And He did it for you.

Jesus loves you.

Jesus sees you.

And the battle you're facing, no matter how dark it feels, isn't hopeless.

I'm praying you remember this as you go to sleep tonight, sweet friend.

Light will find a way to win.

SOMETHING TO RELEASE BACK TO GOD FROM TODAY:

_____

_____

A PRAYER TO RECEIVE BEFORE TOMORROW:

Father God, thank You for reminding me of who You are in my circumstances. I pray tonight that You would allow Your truth to soak into the places of my heart that are weary and doubting. I love You, Lord. I'm trusting You with every outcome and uncertainty. In Jesus' name, amen.

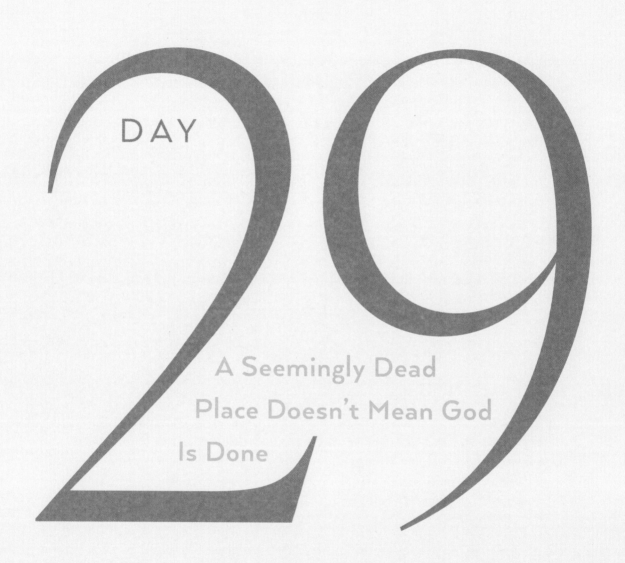

DAY

29

A Seemingly Dead
Place Doesn't Mean God
Is Done

Jesus said to her, "I am the resurrection and the life."

JOHN 11:25

MORNING

I noticed something this morning as I passed by a flower on my favorite bike path.

What seemed void of any evidence of possibility yesterday was suddenly stirring with life today. A small flower had broken through the impossibly hard asphalt and bloomed with glorious color.

I needed to see this today. I needed to notice this reality. It was like God Himself stopped me in my tracks to see this and teach me something.

In my heart, I know God often does His most powerful work in the unseen places. But when I'm waiting to see Him move in a painful family situation I'm dealing with or a prayer request I've continued to cry out about, the mystery around His unseen activity feels cruel, not loving.

But here's what that little blooming flower reminded me today about God: whatever He touches, He transforms. An apparent dead place is not beyond the reach of our life-giving God. Just when we're ready to call it quits, God shows up. Just when a situation looks like it's over, God intervenes. Just when something looks too far gone with what we can perceive with our own eyes, God resurrects what looks beyond repair. And just when we acknowledge that some things really do die, God brings purpose from that pain.

God may not give us eyes to see what He's doing in the unseen places. But I believe He'll give us hearts to trust Him.

To trust that He hears our prayers even when they haven't been answered yet in the way we thought the answer would come.

To trust that He's still good even when hurtful situations seem pointless and never-ending.

To trust that He has good plans for our lives even though our futures feel uncertain, scary, and confusing.

Just when we're ready to name something dead, I can hear God saying, *Not until I say so. This is part of the story, but it isn't the full story.*

A statement to remember as I walk into today:

An apparent dead place is not beyond the reach of our life-giving God.

EVENING

Oh, friend, I don't know what devastating circumstances you're walking through that appear like they'll never get any better. But I believe God wants us to embrace a powerful truth before we go to sleep tonight:

Even if our circumstances aren't good, His purpose always is.

We don't have to know all the details. We don't have to know the whys and the hows. But we can trust Jesus will accomplish His purpose.

We may be facing a delay, distraction, or even devastation for a season. But it's not our final destination. Resurrection is coming. For some of us, it could happen miraculously today. For all who trust in Jesus as Savior, whether our circumstances change or not, there's an eternal hope because His resurrection power has the final say.

In eternity, Jesus wins.

Doubt doesn't have the final say. Disease doesn't have the final say. Heartbreak doesn't have the final say. Even death doesn't have the final say. The only one who gets the final say in our lives is Jesus. We can release anything that's weighing heavy in our hearts to the One who is the resurrection and the life. Both today and forever.

SOMETHING TO RELEASE BACK TO GOD FROM TODAY:

_____

_____

A PRAYER TO RECEIVE BEFORE TOMORROW:

Father, thank You for the power You have to resurrect what seems dead back to life. Help me remember that because You have defeated death, there is nothing in my life You do not have the power to defeat. Help me trust You in the area of my life that I'm tempted to believe is too far gone or unrepairable. In Jesus' name, amen.

DAY

30

Choosing Trust
over Taking
Control

Trust in the Lord with all your heart and lean not on your own understanding; in all your ways submit to him, and he will make your paths straight.

PROVERBS 3:5-6

MORNING

God is teaching me so much about really trusting Him.

Fully. Completely. Wholeheartedly.

Though the path I'm on may feel uncertain right now, He's faithful to shed just enough light for me to see the very next step. And this isn't Him being mysterious—this is a great demonstration of His mercy.

Instead of berating Him with my suggestions or projections, clenching my fists and reaching for control, I simply need to embrace the very next thing He shows me. And then the next.

Because here's what I know about myself: if God showed me too much revelation through an exact blueprint of where I was headed and what was exactly taking shape, I might panic if His plan didn't match what I desperately wanted. Or I may be tempted to run ahead of His timing and try to make things happen on my own. On the flip side, if He showed me too little and was completely silent and absent, never revealing Himself or His guidance, I'd be paralyzed with the thought that He'd abandoned me.

In His kindness, God gives each of us just enough revelation to keep going today. Most days this revelation is in the form of an invitation from Him to be fully obedient to Him right now. If I read a Scripture verse, I can feel a prodding in my heart: *Lysa, are you being obedient to Me in this?* Or as I listen to wise counsel, I am challenged: *Lysa, are you willing to implement what is being suggested to you in this situation?* Often my confusion isn't because God is being mysterious; it's because I'm not being obedient.

As I enter this brand-new day, I'm seeking Him rather than trying to figure out His plan. Instead of filling the gaps of the unknown with my suggestions to God, I'm placing my trust in God. I want to invite you to join me.

Friend, that thing you need to trust God with? He's trustworthy enough to handle it and hold you tightly in the process.

We don't have to know it all to trust Him completely. We can take it one day at a time. One step at a time. One act of obedience at a time. One sliver of light at a time.

Even if you can't see the whole pathway forward, trust that goodness is ahead. Cling to His truth, and let God light the way step-by-step.

Let's not let fears about tomorrow steal our joy for today. Let's determine today to be seekers of the light and vessels of joy.

A statement to remember as I walk into today: ||||·|||

Let's not let fears about tomorrow steal our joy for today.

EVENING

As God is inviting me to trust Him more, I'm discovering this: I'm acknowledging God is in control, and I'm freeing myself from carrying the weight of trying to do it all.

I can release my desire for control, my attachment to outcomes, my never-ending questions, doubts, and fears . . . all into the hands of the God who is always faithful. The God who personally goes before me. The God who never leaves us to figure it all out on our own.

The more I trust Him to do what only He can do, the less I will resist Him. The less I resist Him, the less I will suffer with anxiety about the unknown.

Our God, help us trust You with it all. Help us see that we're going to make it. And help us sleep peacefully because You've got it all under control.

SOMETHING TO RELEASE BACK TO GOD FROM TODAY:

_____

_____

A PRAYER TO RECEIVE BEFORE TOMORROW:

Father God, thank You for reminding me that I don't have to have all the answers. I just need to trust You. Help me to fix my eyes on Your faithfulness. I'm loosening my grip and surrendering all my life into Your loving and capable hands. In Jesus' name, amen.

DAY

31

I'm Not
Really
Sure the
Lord Is
with Me

Blessed are the pure in heart, for they will see God.

MATTHEW 5:8

MORNING

I didn't want to say it. I didn't want to feel it. I didn't want to be struggling with it. Yet I know it's impossible to fix problems I refuse to admit I have.

I'm not sure the Lord is really with me.

I was in a season where I'd been doing church for a long time. But I kept having this suspicion that other Christians had a more direct line to God than I had.

Things just seemed to work out for them. They kept gratitude journals and had plenty to write on those pages every day. And when we would study the Bible together, they had incredible revelations that they'd express by saying, "These verses really spoke to my heart." "The Lord showed me something amazing." Or, "I see His hand moving so powerfully in my life right now."

I would hear their confidence and want to quietly pack up my notes and Bible—which didn't have nearly the amount of highlight marks in it as theirs did—and just go home. What was I missing?

Sometimes I would feel a rush of assurance and comfort when standing with my hands raised in a crowd electric with praise songs. Or I'd have a rare moment when something big happened and I could declare, "Wow, look what the Lord did!" But I wasn't like those other girls at Bible study. And I was too afraid to admit my uncertainty to anyone or ask questions.

I just kept quiet. And I tried to have the same unwavering spiritual confidence that everyone else had. All the while, I couldn't shake the nagging thoughts: *If Jesus really cares about me, why does He seem to stay hidden from me? If Jesus really wants a relationship with me, why can't I see Him, hear Him, and get to know Him?* I mean, if a human relationship was this mysterious, I'd assume the person was ghosting me, rejecting me, and giving me the not-so-subtle hint to move on.

Then I remembered some relationship advice I'd heard: if people want to improve their connections with friends and family, they need to communicate their desires more clearly.

Maybe that's what I needed to do with Jesus. I wrote in my journal three desires I had for my relationship with Jesus: 1. *Jesus, I want to see You.* 2. *Jesus, I want to hear You.* 3. *Jesus, I want to know You.*

At first, this felt so odd. After all, I knew I wouldn't likely physically see or hear Jesus. But my heart was crying out to see evidence of His reality in my life. I wanted to experience His presence and walk in the assurance that He saw me, heard me, and wanted to know me.

Then I read the words of Matthew 5:8: "Blessed are the pure in heart, for they will see God."

This verse doesn't say only a perfect person will see God. No, the pure in heart—the one who really wants to pursue God—will see Him.

I kept journaling about this and then one day decided to turn that list into a prayer I prayed each day. Eventually I added, "I want to follow hard after You every day so before my feet hit the floor, I say yes to You." I decided that I would also start looking for Him with greater intentionality throughout my day. I would tune in to my own life experiences and start living with expectation of this prayer being answered.

It's now been over twenty years since I started praying this prayer.

And I'm different because of learning to practice the presence of Jesus and experiencing Him daily. It has been an intentional, daily pursuit of Him. Looking for Him in unexpected places. Through the good. Through the not-so-good. And everything in between.

I still think about the doubt that haunted me in my early days of following Christ: *I'm not sure the Lord is really with me.* I can't say that doubt doesn't ever creep back in my mind. But what has dramatically changed is that it doesn't send me spiraling into panic and hopelessness now. I'm not afraid doubt is a sign that my faith is weak. Quite the opposite. I now realize that doubt is an invitation to start looking for the Lord with even more intentionality.

I want to remind you of words from Day 23 before we wrap up this morning.

God isn't hiding from us; He's waiting to be seen by us.

How might you look for Jesus today?

A statement to remember as I walk into today:

Doubt is an invitation to start looking for the Lord with even more intentionality.

EVENING

If you're desperate for God's intervention in your story, oh sweet friend, I understand.

I can't give you a save-the-date of when to expect the arrival of God's breakthrough, but I can remind you again with wisdom I've learned in my own life.

We don't serve a do-nothing God. He is always working.

One of my favorite stories in the Bible is the story of Joseph in the book of Genesis. He walked through years of rejection, false accusation, and wrongful imprisonment, and he was seemingly forgotten . . . but with God, there is always a "meanwhile." God was bringing about something only He could do with the circumstances before Joseph. He was positioning Joseph and preparing him to be used to help save the lives of millions of people during a famine that would have otherwise destroyed multiple nations.

God is always doing something.

On this side of eternity we don't always get to see how God is working in our most painful experiences. But we can let the way God worked in Joseph's story be a reminder of His faithfulness in our stories.

I now look back at different situations in my life and think, *Wow, there was never one moment when God was doing nothing.*

Friend, the heartbreaks you carry are enormous. And if no one else has ever said this to you, I want to: I'm so sorry for what you've been through. Your hurt matters. Not only do I care about you, but so does God.

Before you go to sleep tonight, don't miss the tremendous amount of tenderness in the words of 1 Peter 5:7: "casting all your cares [all your anxieties, all your worries, and all your concerns, once and for all] on Him, for He cares about you [with deepest affection, and watches over you very carefully]" (AMP).

Keep trusting Him. Keep training your eyes to look for God. He sees you. He loves you. And He knows exactly what needs to happen in every detail of your story. You do not serve a do-nothing God.

SOMETHING TO RELEASE BACK TO GOD FROM TODAY:

_____

_____

A PRAYER TO RECEIVE BEFORE TOMORROW:

Father God, I confess that sometimes I forget to remember Your faithfulness from the past, especially when I am overwhelmed with unpredictable things today. Keep reminding me that not only do You see me, but You love me. I don't know exactly what tomorrow will look like, but I do know who I'll be looking to—You, Lord—whose love is unfailing and whose hand is the safest place to entrust my hope. In Jesus' name, amen.

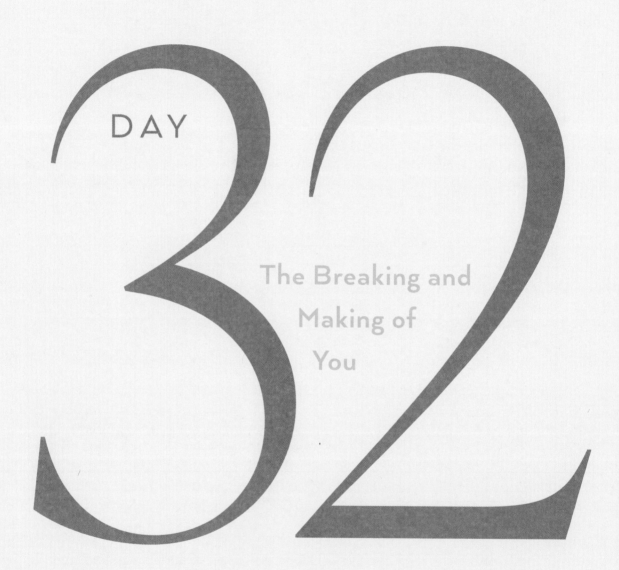

DAY

32

The Breaking and
Making of
You

> You intended to harm me, but God intended it for good to
> accomplish what is now being done, the saving of many lives.
>
> GENESIS 50:20

MORNING

Something beautifully striking holds my attention when I think about the creation story. Jesus was *there*!

And He wasn't just there; He was creating. John 1:3 reveals, "Through him [Jesus] all things were made." The light, sky, water, land, plants, sun, moon, stars, and all animals.

I've always pictured God creating all things and then Jesus using creation in His teachings in the Gospels. But now I'm rethinking that. I wonder if Jesus knew what He wanted to teach, so He created the exact right illustrations. For example, did He create the birds in the beginning and then thousands of years later cue the birds when He walked the earth as a human and taught lessons using these intentionally created creatures?

There is great intentionality with every detail of everything He touches. Purpose is woven into every created thing, and though you may struggle to believe it sometimes, you are no exception.

Here's how I know: look at Genesis 1:26. After creating the world and all living things, God said, "Let us make mankind in our image, in our likeness." And at that moment, you were thought of with great intentionality. Every bit of who you are, what you are meant to be, and the incredible purpose you are meant to fulfill had Jesus' full thought and creative touch.

Psalm 139:16 says, "Your eyes saw my unformed body; all the days ordained for me were written in your book before one of them came to be." Oh, the patience it must have taken for Him to wait all this time to bring your version of love, personality, and unique gifts into the world!

But now that you're here, you better believe He's got creative plans for you.

And as confusing as it may be, God can use even the hard and heartbreaking realities of our lives to shape our characters to match our callings. I see this so clearly in the life of Joseph, who was quoted in our key verse today. God didn't cause Joseph's hardships. But God did use the hardships Joseph walked through to equip him for his calling and point him toward his purpose.

And the same can be true in our lives as well.

So today, look for Him and accept the invitation to participate and cooperate with Him. Maybe that tough situation you're facing won't be the breaking of you but rather the making of you—a stronger and more capable you necessary for you to live out your calling.

Purpose is woven into every created thing, and though you may struggle to believe it sometimes, you are no exception.

EVENING

Before we go to sleep, I want us to come together and make one really important decision: we will keep our minds and hearts focused on the truth-filled words of God no matter what.

You see, the Enemy wants us to feel exposed in areas we already feel insecure. And his lies and accusations often sneak up in the moments we're trying to make progress in an assignment God has put in front of us. So I want us to be extra committed and attentive to fixing our thoughts on things that are true.

If at any point you hear lies from the Enemy sneaking up that sound like *If only you were . . .* or *Why can't you just . . .* or *If you were only more like her . . .* , remember our marked moment right here. Reject those words and instead reach for truth.

Friend, we must let God's Word become the words of our stories—and the only truth-filled words we allow to shape who we are and what we believe about ourselves.

The truth is, you are brilliant and special and amazing in a million different ways. God knows you completely, loves you fully, and perfectly orchestrated all the good that can come from what you walk through in life. He wants your heart so He can show you everything He has for you.

Release those lies the Enemy is trying to get you to believe so you can go to sleep embracing the truth that sets you free.

SOMETHING TO RELEASE BACK TO GOD FROM TODAY:

_____

_____

Jesus, thank You for thinking of me from the very beginning of creation. I'm so grateful for Your intentional design in the way You made me. Help me release any lies that are opposite to the truth of what Your Word says about who I am. I want Your words to be the only words that make up my identity. In Jesus' name, amen.

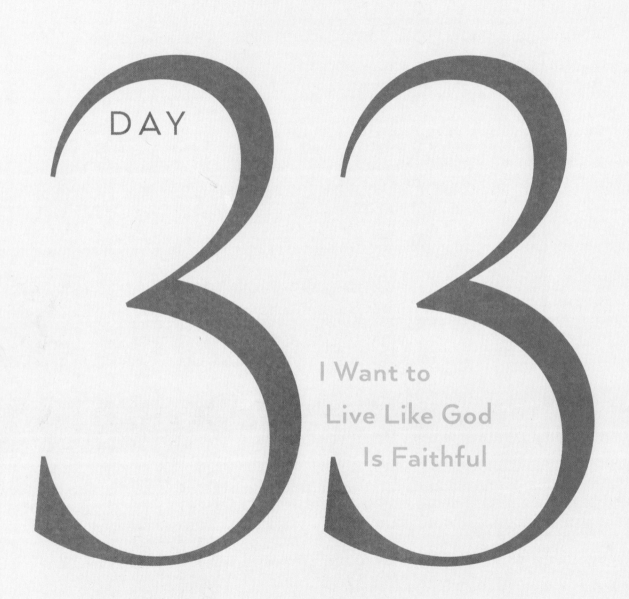

DAY

33

I Want to
Live Like God
Is Faithful

> Because of the LORD's great love we are not
> consumed, for his compassions never fail. They are
> new every morning; great is your faithfulness.
>
> LAMENTATIONS 3:22-23

MORNING

One of the quickest ways to get discouraged and disillusioned with the faithfulness of God is to look to people and circumstances as the determining factors.

People will fail you. Circumstances will falter. We have days where life events shake us and break us and make us question, "Why? Why this? Why now?" We live in a fallen world where fallen things happen, and there's evil among us. It hurts in horrific ways.

But God's faithfulness doesn't diminish in the face of hard realities.

He rises. He lifts. He shifts us, and He settles us in places of deeper trust. He takes us by the hand and whispers, *No matter what, I've got this. I've got you. And I'll hold on to you forever.*

God is faithful. And today I want to live like I *really* believe it. Therefore, I need to speak it out loud and live it out loud. Even in circumstances that make my heart hurt.

If you woke up to something challenging today, I understand, sweet friend. But here's what I know: We may cry. We may weep. But by the grace of God, we can also grab one another's hands and stand. Together. Proclaiming truth.

I wish we were sharing coffee and processing all these things together today. This is what I would remind you: Heaven is closer than we think. Evil is in the process of being defeated. Therefore, we can stare at heartbreak and pain, and though we are crying, we can still be walking in absolute victory. God's faithfulness and mercy never change and never fail; in fact, they are new this morning. While there may be uncertainty around us, we can cling to that certain truth and get up to face today.

Now, let's live like He's faithful. Because He is.

A statement to remember as I walk into today:

God's faithfulness doesn't diminish in the face of hard realities.

EVENING

I know how hard it can be to proclaim God's faithfulness in prayer when you feel like you have more questions than answers, more doubts than assurances, and more unanswered prayers than tangible breakthroughs.

If you find yourself there tonight, I want you to remember this: God already knows what we need before we ask Him. We pray not because God needs our suggestions.

We pray because we don't truly know what we need.

We pray because He sees the bigger picture, while we see only a sliver.

We pray because we have limited perspectives, limited thoughts, and limited views.

We pray because we need so much more than quick fixes and help for our troubles.

We pray because we need Him.

Even though it feels more complicated than that, it really is that simple. And we must remember that our level of faith in our current situations doesn't diminish His level of faithfulness.

Faithfulness is not something God does or doesn't do. He is faithful regardless of what we're facing. So pray what you need to pray. Or simply say, "God, I don't know what I need or what to ask for, but You do. Please help me."

Friend, your prayers are heard by a forever-faithful God. Rest assured of this tonight as you fall asleep.

SOMETHING TO RELEASE BACK TO GOD FROM TODAY:

_____

_____

A PRAYER TO RECEIVE BEFORE TOMORROW:

God, I know You're so faithful through every situation and circumstance I face. I pray for a heart that grows to trust that You're faithful even when I experience doubts and pain or am waiting for breakthrough in hard situations. I love You, Lord. I hand over to You everything that feels heavy in my heart right now. Give me courage to live like You're faithful. In Jesus' name, amen.

DAY

34

Make
Compassion
Your Legacy

> Be kind and compassionate to one another, forgiving
> each other, just as in Christ God forgave you.
>
> EPHESIANS 4:32

MORNING

When the excruciating pain you feel in your heart goes unattended for an extended period of time, it's easy to let your heart grow cynical and less compassionate.

Maybe you've experienced a significant job loss recently or you're going through a breakup. Or you just got a heartbreaking medical diagnosis. Or you're in the depths of an adoption journey that's included unexpected delays. Maybe you're trying to move forward after a betrayal from someone close to you, or one of your kids is walking through something really difficult, and the heartbreak just gets more and more heavy.

Friend, I understand.

And I don't want to make light of anything you're walking through right now.

Your pain is real. Your tears matter. Your hurt doesn't go unseen.

But I do want to share something to encourage you today. You may be experiencing pain in your story *right now*, but that doesn't mean this pain will make up the whole story of your life. It doesn't have to be the story you tell forever or even the story you're known for.

You see, when we allow the pain we've experienced to make us more compassionate toward others, we get to change the narrative that pain begs to write.

We may not get to choose what happens to us. And we don't get to choose how our stories always end. But we get to choose the type of person we become regardless of any outcome.

A person of hope.

A person of encouragement.

A person of kindness.

A person of compassion.

We may experience heartbreaking situations, but we can still be known for beautiful qualities like compassion. Compassion doesn't mean we're overlooking the harsh reality of things we're facing or stuffing feelings we need to process. Actually, some of the most compassionate people I know have experienced the deepest pain. They've chosen to let it make them more compassionate people in the process.

Today, we get to choose. We can choose to live out words like Ephesians 4:32, "Be kind and compassionate to one another, forgiving each other, just as in Christ God forgave you," and

Colossians 3:12, "Therefore, as God's chosen people, holy and dearly loved, clothe yourselves with compassion, kindness, humility, gentleness and patience."

I want to be known for these things. I want to fill my life with these God-honoring qualities. I want my legacy to be compassion.

And I want this for you too. Today is a great day to send an encouraging text message. Smile at a stranger who looks like she's hurting. Offer to pick up your friend's kids from school. Listen with your full, undivided attention. Bring someone at work her favorite coffee or drink.

These are just a few ways we can color today with compassion.

This chapter of your life may be painful, but that's not all it is. I love you, friend. Let's make today one to remember.

A statement to remember as I walk into today:

You may be experiencing pain in your story right now, but that doesn't mean this pain will make up the whole story of your life.

EVENING

When people break your heart, don't let them also steal your future.

There is a time to grieve.

But then, there is a time to laugh again, make cookies, go to new places, and slide down a slide with those who need to see you moving on and living again.

Maybe this rejection was really a protection of new joys that may never have been if the person had stayed. Maybe this rejection is a protection in disguise. Maybe this rejection is a redirection toward a more God-honoring future.

This is an end to what could have been. Yes. But it's also a new beginning. Stay with God. Keep praying. Get in His Word. Stay close to people who encourage you in these things.

And you'll soon see that God has already prepared something beautiful on the other side of your grief.

With that said, maybe it's time to release back to God what we can't change so we can discover what He has for us now.

As you go to sleep tonight, ask God to give you eyes to see goodness in the possibilities of what's ahead. I know it's beautiful. I know it's good. I know because I know Him.

Love you, friend.

SOMETHING TO RELEASE BACK TO GOD FROM TODAY:

_____

_____

A PRAYER TO RECEIVE BEFORE TOMORROW:

Jesus, thank You for walking with me through the hardships I've experienced. I have a deep desire for You to keep my heart soft so I can be a person marked by compassion. Even though hurtful things have happened to me, I don't want to be known for those things. I want to be known for the forgiveness and healing You have instilled in me. Give me an opportunity to extend compassion to someone who needs to see You moving in her life this week. In Jesus' name, amen.

DAY

35

How
Do I Know
God Is Doing
Something?

> Since they would not accept my advice and spurned my rebuke, they will eat the fruit of their ways and be filled with the fruit of their schemes.
>
> PROVERBS 1:30–31

MORNING

A few years ago, I was walking through the ending of a very traumatic relationship. Everything felt hard, unfair, and quite honestly like God wasn't doing what I assumed a good God should do. The choices of this other person were hurting not only me but also many others I loved deeply. I remember being so confused when it appeared like God was doing nothing.

When I look back on that season now, I realize and can more clearly recognize God was absolutely working things out for me. He was working in unseen places.

There is a book in the Bible where God's name is not mentioned even one time. When I first read this book, that fact surprised me. But what I realize now is God's presence was there, just as God's presence is here now with whatever we are facing. It's just that sometimes God does incredible moves without calling any attention to Himself at all.

In the book of Esther, an evil man named Haman plotted to kill the Jewish people. As you read through this story, it seems like Haman is getting away with his evil intentions and God isn't intervening to change it. The whole book is ten chapters, and by the end of chapter 5, things seem to be hopeless and going in favor of Haman. He had convinced the king to sign an order for the Jewish people to be killed. It seemed evil was winning.

But then in chapter 6, something kept the king awake one night, which prompted him to have the history of his reign read to him. That's when the king realized a Jewish man had helped save his life. Long story short, the very way Haman had plotted to have this Jewish man killed was the way Haman died. He ate the fruit of his own wicked schemes.

The comforting part to me is that I feel certain God had a hand in making sure the king didn't sleep and that he was reminded of the kindness of the Jewish man.

Not only was this Jewish man honored, but Haman was the very one made to honor this man he despised. Haman's pride backfired, and his evil intentions led to his own humiliation.

Then Esther was granted time with the king, her husband. She didn't demand it. She didn't rush it. But in the right way, she requested it. Then she was able to ask that the king spare her life and the lives of her people. And through that conversation, Haman's evil intentions were exposed.

No human could have possibly arranged for all that to happen.

The people honored God with what they could do. Esther certainly did her part, as did many others. But they didn't do the wrong things to try and bring about the right things.

Doing things God's way and in God's timing is the right way and the right timing. Our job in whatever we are facing is to keep our hearts pure and trust we will see God.

Doing things God's way and in God's timing is the right way and the right timing.

EVENING

Many times throughout Scripture when sin is mentioned, it's coupled with being unaware or blinded by our own desires or a hardening of the heart. Hebrews 3:12–13 reminds us of this: "See to it, brothers and sisters, that none of you has a sinful, unbelieving heart that turns away from the living God. But encourage one another daily, as long as it is called 'Today,' so that none of you may be hardened by sin's deceitfulness."

In this morning's reading, Haman's sin blinded him, made him hard-hearted, and eventually caught up with him because that's what sin always does. Tonight, as you go to sleep, release any simmering resentments and desires for retaliation against others. Ask God to show you what you need to do. Then trust that while your heart stays pure, He will do what only He can do. He will address the sins someone has committed against you. He will handle what we would only mishandle. Only He is able to carry the weight of vengeance balanced with justice and mercy.

SOMETHING TO RELEASE BACK TO GOD FROM TODAY:

_____

_____

Heavenly Father, purify my heart tonight. I trust You to handle any and all outcomes that I feel unsure of or overwhelmed by. Help me to be obedient to You. I want to walk in step with You, Your ways, and Your timing. In Jesus' name, amen.

DAY 36

Making Room for Slow Days and Still Moments

He says, "Be still, and know that I am God."

PSALM 46:10

MORNING

Sometimes in the midst of a crazy season and the rush of a Monday in the middle of the summer, I just need to sit for a few moments.

Quiet the to-do list.

Still the hurry.

Shush the worry.

Unrush.

Slow days are a choice. And slow days are good for the soul.

When you're trying to heal and move forward, don't underestimate the number of slow days your tender heart may need.

Sometimes in the rush of busy days with a lot to distract us from feeling the pain, we are tempted to believe that because we are keeping up, we must be okay. But just coping, pushing through, and numbing the pain isn't the same thing as healing the pain. Slow moments where we acknowledge the pain we are feeling helps point us in the direction of healing. We must feel the pain to deal with the pain and eventually heal the pain.

Look at the way physical healing takes place in our body. Physical pain drives us to get the necessary help we need. Physical pain reminds us that we may need more rest, we may need to walk with a limp for a while, we may need ongoing treatment, and we may need to take time off until the intensity of the pain isn't so crippling. If you've ever tended to an open wound, you know it heals slowly, day by day, and it must be tended to at each stage of healing. Emotional pain works the same way—it's just harder to see and harder to discern why slowing down is so important.

Healing is both a choice and a process. When we want to heal, we must allow ourselves time to walk through the necessary process. Now, obviously, it won't be realistic for most of us to stop working and peace out on our responsibilities. But we can recognize this isn't a season to take on extra projects or be the super volunteer. We can get intentional about communicating to our family and friends our need to be slower during our off days to rest, reflect, read, and regroup. And most of all, we need time to cry out to Jesus and ask Him for the strength and perspectives we will need to walk through this.

I believe some of the most important days we'll experience will be the slow days filled with still moments with Jesus.

So, before this day gets started, let's take a moment to whisper these words together:

I love You, Jesus. I need You, Jesus. I trust You, Jesus. I need You to show me what I need to see today, Jesus. I believe You are walking with me and will lead me. Now I'm going to sit quietly and listen to You. I'm going to still my body, and I'm asking You to comfort my heart and unrush my mind.

A statement to remember as I walk into today:

Some of the most important days we'll experience will be slow days filled with still moments listening to Jesus.

EVENING

One of the biggest lessons God taught me this year is to spend less time making suggestions and more time listening in prayer.

That's one of the beautifully challenging parts of still moments.

I'm so prone to want to figure everything out and then tell God, "Bless all this, but please don't mess with all this!"

God begs me to open my hands in surrender instead of hurrying through my list of grand suggestions and projections. The still moments *still* me.

Oh, Lord, forgive me.

I've seen over and over that God's plans are always, always, always better. Before we go to sleep tonight, let's release some of those suggestions and just be still.

Still long enough to embrace the sacred space of simple trust in an all-knowing and loving God.

Still long enough to listen for something God may want to personally speak to us.

Still long enough to lay our heads on our pillows and remember we're not in control—and that's actually a really good thing.

SOMETHING TO RELEASE BACK TO GOD FROM TODAY:

_____

_____

A PRAYER TO RECEIVE BEFORE TOMORROW:

Father God, I am making a decision today to spend more time in prayer and less time hurrying through the demands of my busy schedule. I am resolving not to let the daily tasks and responsibilities of life get in the way of important moments with You. Help me find time to be still in prayer, long enough to hear You speak to me personally. In Jesus' name, amen.

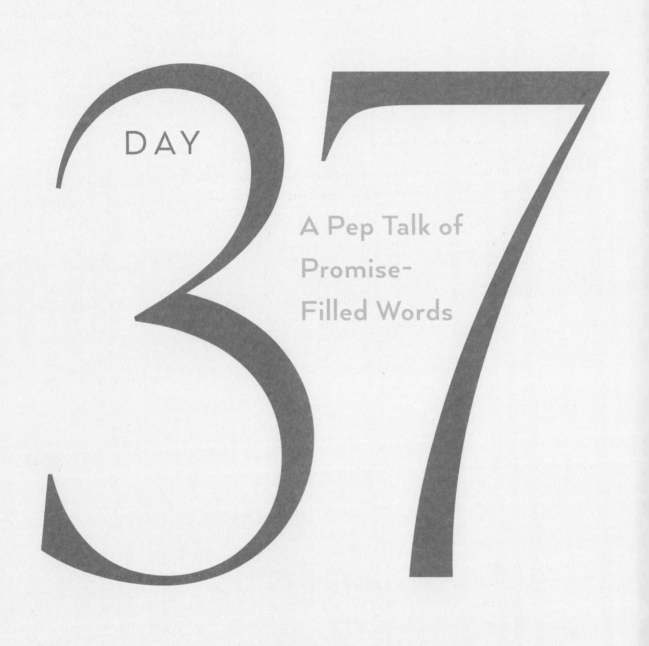

DAY 37

A Pep Talk of
Promise-
Filled Words

And we know that in all things God works for the good of those who
love him, who have been called according to his purpose.

ROMANS 8:28

MORNING

Good morning, friend. We've made some progress through the pages of this book together. We've made honest confessions. We've opened our hands to receive God's truth-filled words. We've released the things we can't control. We've encouraged each other as we've bravely continued to march forward in faith that we *will* make it.

Even if you don't see it, you *are* healing. I know it can be tempting to doubt it, but today is another step forward. The longer I live, the more I see healing less as a destination and more of a daily choice. In case your heart is feeling a little weary this morning, I hope you'll feel a little more encouraged that you're not alone and your beautiful, unique story is still unfolding. The circumstances of today are part of your story, but they are not the whole story.

I thought you may need a pep talk today because I know what it's like to

- start to wonder if these hard situations will be never-ending.
- feel that the hurt will last forever.
- question if you'll survive this time of suffering and come out on the other side.
- process even more devastating news that makes your mind race, your throat tighten, and your eyes swell with tears.
- try to pray in moments where God feels incredibly distant.

I understand. Sometimes all this pain can feel so very pointless.

Over the last couple of years, I've had to face one hardship after another. At many points I've wondered how I would make it through. Even today, I'm still very much in process. Yes, I've done the hard heart work with my counselor and processed all the things with my closest friends. I've been healing. I've gained perspective and understanding for how to move forward. I've made progress. But none of that changes the deep heartbreak I went through.

The reality is, sometimes it still stings. And when that pain bubbles back to the surface, I wonder why God doesn't just take it all away. Wasn't it enough that I had to suffer through the trauma? Why do I have to now suffer with random memories that pop into my brain and cause me to face the loss over and over again?

It's hard to always feel confident in the goodness of God when parts of our story don't at all feel good.

But friend, whether you're trying to make sense of relational fallout, processing fresh grief, or just opening this book desperate for a few moments of encouragement before the day ahead, there's something so very important God wants you and me to know: He is near to us in our heartbreak, and He cares about our despair. Past, present, and future, God is still here.

Right this very minute, in the middle of our own difficult circumstances, we get to choose to cling to truth harder than ever before. We can allow hope to be infused into even the most impossible-looking circumstances. And when we do, we let the devil know he has messed with the wrong girl this time. We can command our weary hearts to remember God is in charge and we are not, and that's a freeing place to be.

As you wrestle this morning with it all—the progress made, the steps forward still to endure, the painful, time-consuming, beautifully refining process that healing is—I want to whisper fresh encouragement to you.

Redemption can still be your story even if it doesn't look the way you thought it would. God is not done, and none of this will be wasted.

Before you close this book and head out for your day, I want us to read a few verses in Romans 8 that are so comforting to me. Every time I read them, I'm reminded I can simply surrender my heart all over again to Jesus and trust Him with every part of the journey I'm on.

The more I surrender to trusting the Lord, rather than trying to make my own way through this, the less I will suffer.

> In the same way, the Spirit helps us in our weakness. We do not know what we ought to pray for, but the Spirit himself intercedes for us through wordless groans. And he who searches our hearts knows the mind of the Spirit, because the Spirit intercedes for God's people in accordance with the will of God. And we know that in all things God works for the good of those who love him, who have been called according to his purpose. (Romans 8:26–28)

A statement to remember as I walk into today:

Redemption can still be your story even if it doesn't look the way you thought it would.

EVENING

Before you go to sleep tonight, I want to challenge you to do something.

This morning I gave you a pep talk filled with encouragement and promises from God. But I would imagine there's someone in your life who needs to be reminded of these words tonight before she goes to sleep.

It doesn't have to be fancy or formal. It doesn't even have to be perfectly worded, but I want you to reach out to whomever God places on your heart right now. Ask God who needs a reminder that He loves her before this day ends.

Okay, do you have her name?

Now, open up a new text and craft a few simple sentences to encourage her heart. I don't know her specific situation or what difficulties she may be facing right now. Maybe you don't know all of the details either, but you know she's hurting. That's okay; the details aren't what matters. If you're feeling uncertain about what to say, borrow some words from God's Word as you remind one more precious soul that she's going to make it:

- "The LORD your God is with you, the Mighty Warrior who saves. He will take great delight in you; in his love he will no longer rebuke you, but will rejoice over you with singing" (Zephaniah 3:17).
- "The LORD will fight for you; you need only to be still" (Exodus 14:14).
- "The LORD is trustworthy in all he promises and faithful in all he does. The LORD upholds all who fall and lifts up all who are bowed down" (Psalm 145:13–14).

I hope I get to hear the stories that came out of this exercise tonight. I know heaven is rejoicing as we're grabbing each other by the hand, clinging to the truth-filled words inside God's Word, and marching forward together.

Sweet dreams, friend.

SOMETHING TO RELEASE BACK TO GOD FROM TODAY:

_____

_____

Jesus, thank You for reminding me of Your promises today. My weary heart needed to be encouraged that You haven't left me, You still have a plan, and healing is possible for me. Put someone on my heart who also needs to be reminded of these things. In Jesus' name, amen.

DAY

38

Sweeping
Our Hearts
Clean with
Forgiveness

> Bear with each other and forgive one another
> if any of you has a grievance against someone.
> Forgive as the Lord forgave you.
>
> COLOSSIANS 3:13

MORNING

I am a soul who likes the concept of forgiveness . . . until I am a hurting soul who doesn't.

Left to my own deep woundedness, forgiveness can seem offensive, impossible, and one of the quickest ways to compound the unfairness of being wronged. I cry for fairness. I want blessings for those who follow the rules of life and love. I want correction for those who break them.

Is that too much to ask?

And it's that exact spot where I like to park, stew, focus on everyone else's wrongs, and rally those who agree with me to join in and help me justify staying right there.

It's like the time in college I stayed in the parking lot of a beautiful vacation spot just to make a point. A small offense happened with my friends on the drive up. When we got to our destination, they all piled out of the car and spent the day making incredible memories together. All the while, I walked around the parking lot with vigilante strides in the sweltering heat, letting my anger intensify with every passing hour.

I relished the idea of teaching my friends a lesson by staging this solo protest. But, in the end, I was the only one affected by it. I'm the only one who missed out on the fun. I'm the one who rode home in silence, knowing no one had been punished by my choices but me.

Please know, I want to acknowledge that much of the pain you and I have been through is much more complicated and devastating than that day at the beach. But in all my offenses, both big and small, I've learned to recognize these soldiers of unforgiveness:

- *Bitterness* masquerades as a high court judge, making me believe I must protect the evidence against all those who hurt me so I can state and restate my airtight case and hear "guilty" proclaimed over the offender. In reality, though, it's a punishing sentence of isolation, out to starve my soul of life-giving relationships.
- *Resentment* cloaks itself in a banner marked with the word *vindication*, making me believe that the only way to get free of my pain is to make sure those who caused it hurt as badly as I do. In reality, though, it's a trap in disguise, with dagger teeth digging into *me*, keeping me tortured and unable to move forward.

- *Trust issues* disguise themselves as private investigators, making me believe they will help me catch everyone out to hurt me and prove that no one is truly honest. In reality, trust issues are toxic gas that, instead of keeping away the few who shouldn't be trusted, choke the life out of everyone who gets close to me.

These are the soldiers of unforgiveness that have waged war against me. The soldiers of unforgiveness are waging war right now against every hurting person.

They are the ones who will always lead us to isolation, the emotional darkness of broken relationships, spiritual darkness with heaped-on shame, and a darkened outlook where we are unable to see the beauty that awaits just beyond the parking lot.

What if I'd been able to release the offense and move forward that day at the beach? What if we could all do that? I'm not talking about excusing abuse or allowing someone to traumatize us. I'm talking about small offenses that we refuse to address properly.

This isn't about diminishing what we've been through or making light of the anguish we've cried a million tears over. It's knowing that those who cooperate most fully with forgiveness are those who dance most freely in the beauty of redemption. And what exactly is this beautiful redemption?

Redemption is sweeping our hearts clean of little offenses before they cause us big problems. And it's finally finding the freedom to move on. Isn't that what so many of us really want?

We don't have to stay stuck here, friend. Forgiveness is the weapon. Our choices moving forward are the battlefield. Being released from that heavy feeling is the reward. Regaining the possibility of trust and closeness is the sweet victory. And walking confidently with the Lord from hurt to healing is the freedom that awaits.

Now, let's go live this beautiful day ahead.

A statement to remember as I walk into today:

Redemption is sweeping our hearts clean of little offenses before they cause us big problems.

I often want to see the good God promises right now, but sometimes God's good answer is "not yet." Ugh. This is so hard for me.

I know how incredibly hard it can be to be in a place of wondering and waiting. I think these places are often where unforgiveness can creep in. The longer we beg and wait for God to fix this situation or this family member or that conversation, the more our patience grows thin, and our hearts can get crowded with the very things for which we really don't want to be known: Controlling. Manipulative. Untrusting. Bitter. Resentful.

But here's what I've discovered: God has perfect timing for everything. And remembering this helps keep my heart swept clean. You see, remembering and trusting God's timing to be perfect reminds me of the humbling truth that God is God, and I am not. His timing is not my timing. His ways are not my ways. It's not just about releasing those little offenses between us and others. I also want to keep my heart swept clean for any offense I may secretly be holding against God right now.

Sweet friend, God's promises are still in process for you. Right now. Even in circumstances where you can't see any evidence of good yet.

Keep holding on. God isn't done with your story. Release the need to know it all and control it all simply by just whispering, "Jesus, I trust You. Keep my heart swept clean. I know Your promises for me are in process. I want to be ready to be used by You."

Remember, "not yet" doesn't mean "not ever." God's got this.

And with that, you can sleep peacefully.

SOMETHING TO RELEASE BACK TO GOD FROM TODAY:

_____

_____

A PRAYER TO RECEIVE BEFORE TOMORROW:

Father God, thank You for forgiving me of my sins. Because of my awareness today of how much I've been forgiven in my own life, help me extend forgiveness more freely to other people. Soften my heart and purify me of any bitterness and resentment. In Jesus' name, amen.

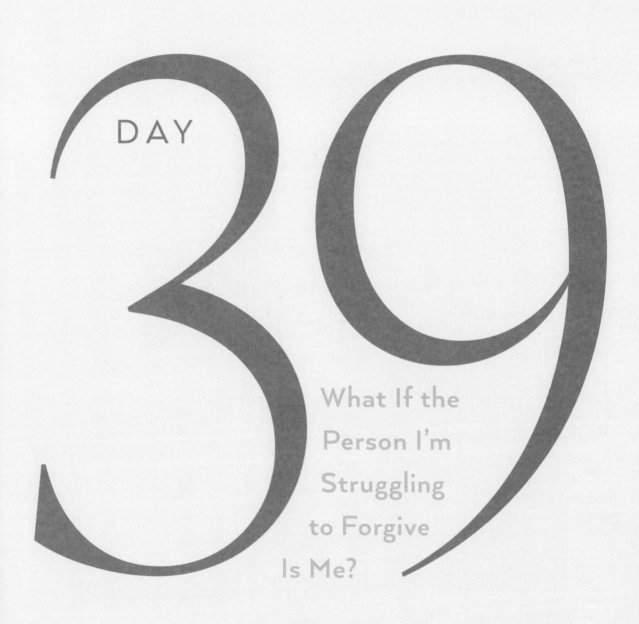

DAY

39

What If the
Person I'm
Struggling
to Forgive
Is Me?

Then I acknowledged my sin to you and did not cover up my iniquity. I said, "I will confess my transgressions to the Lord." And you forgave the guilt of my sin.

PSALM 32:5

MORNING

Yesterday we talked about keeping our hearts swept clean from offenses with others and maybe even hidden resentments toward God.

But do you ever feel like the hardest person to forgive is actually *yourself*?

I understand this. Deeply. I so wish we were sitting together for this conversation.

When I was in my early twenties, I made a decision I wish with everything in me that I could go back and change. I had an abortion. Knowing nothing could be done to reverse that decision filled me with the deepest kind of despair.

Afterward, every time I heard others talking harshly about abortion, I was filled with shame. It felt like a life sentence I would never be healed from.

I would say, "I can't forgive myself." What I meant was, "I don't think forgiveness is possible for a person like me. And I don't think I'll ever be free from the shame of what I've done."

Maybe this is where you are right now—struggling to overcome feelings of shame and regret from choices you wish you could go back and change, and it's keeping you from moving forward and experiencing healing today.

That's why it feels so important to share what I've learned with you. When I researched the concept of forgiving ourselves, I was a little shocked to discover it's not in the Bible. I started to realize that, just as we can't accomplish salvation apart from God, we can't bestow on ourselves forgiveness. Forgiveness starts with God.

Since we are not the judge, we can't pardon ourselves. So when we are struggling with forgiveness for ourselves, what's really happening is a struggle to receive the full forgiveness of God.

Jesus gave His very life to provide forgiveness for our sins, which isn't just *part* of the Christian faith—forgiveness is the very *cornerstone* of the Christian faith. Forgiveness for our sins isn't just a hope we have; it is the greatest reality for all who choose to receive salvation through accepting Jesus as the Lord of their lives.

Often what keeps us from walking as forgiven people is the struggle with feelings of shame and regret. These are very heavy burdens to bear. In my own life, I've carried many burdens. But the weight of shame is by far the heaviest I've ever known.

Shame is a burden God doesn't want any of us carrying. And I'm so thankful for these two things that eventually helped me fully receive His forgiveness and get out from underneath shame's condemning weight:

1. *I needed to have a marked moment confessing, repenting, and asking God for forgiveness.* I couldn't do this by myself. I wanted a witness who could forever remind me that I had asked for God's forgiveness and was, therefore, forgiven. I also verbalized out loud that I received God's forgiveness, so I could have a definite memory of me acknowledging His gift of mercy.
2. *I had to remember that shame and accusation come from the Enemy.* Satan will do everything possible to try to keep us from sharing a testimony of the forgiveness and redemption of Jesus. And the Enemy loves to hold people hostage to shame by making them too afraid to share what they've hidden in the darkness. I was terrified to tell people what I'd done. But I told God I would share my story if ever there was a young girl in danger of making the same uninformed decision as I did. When I eventually let God use my painful choice for good, I started to see glimpses of redemption. Seeing God take what the Enemy meant for evil and use it for good didn't take away my grief, but it started to heal my shame.

Friend, shame and condemnation aren't from God. Confess what you've done. Ask for God's forgiveness today. Receive His forgiveness today. And then walk in His freedom today. You can live the greatest testimony of truth there is—redemption. This is possible for you this morning.

A statement to remember as I walk into today:

Shame is a burden God doesn't want any of us carrying.

EVENING

As we release the weight of shame today, I pray we also let this experience make our hearts tender.

Knowing what it feels like to make a terrible mistake gives us more compassion when others make terrible mistakes. This isn't excusing wrong or hurtful behaviors in the name of compassion. There is time for confronting those behaviors in a conversation filled with grace and truth. There is a time for drawing healthy boundaries and putting in place parameters that keep us safe and our relationships sustainable.

But at the same time, having an attitude of compassion helps us not to shame others.

I know the weight of shame I've carried because of things in my own past, and I don't ever want another human to carry that same awful weight.

Therefore, let's choose our words carefully. When someone makes a mistake, let's make sure we don't forever label her by her mistake. If she is repentant—willing to no longer commit the offense and seeking true forgiveness—she should be allowed the same opportunity for redemption as we have been given.

And even if the person isn't willing to change, unhealthy shame isn't the key that unlocks healthy changes. Shame may guilt a person into making temporary behavior modifications but not bring about the lasting good we really desire for that person. Shame actually makes people feel more and more inclined never to expose their deepest pain to any kind of healing light.

What helped me finally bring my darkness into the light was a kind soul who wove truth and grace through the details of her own past struggle with the exact same sin and shame I was wrestling through. As I saw her healing, I started to believe I could heal as well.

Shame pushes people further into darkness. But our own admission of how desperately we need grace and truth helps people walk toward the same kind of healing we have found.

SOMETHING TO RELEASE BACK TO GOD FROM TODAY:

A PRAYER TO RECEIVE BEFORE TOMORROW:

Jesus, thank You for paying for my sin and shame on the cross. I'm thankful today for a fresh revelation of Your grace and mercy. When the Enemy's accusations come at me, remind me of who I am because of You—forgiven, loved, and whole. In Jesus' name, amen.

DAY 40

I Don't Like Being Caught Off Guard

> "Blessed is the man who trusts in the Lord, whose trust is the Lord. He is like a tree planted by water, that sends out its roots by the stream, and does not fear when heat comes, for its leaves remain green, and is not anxious in the year of drought, for it does not cease to bear fruit."
>
> JEREMIAH 17:7–8 ESV

MORNING

You know how some people love the thrill of being surprised?

They love surprise parties. They would love to show up at work today and learn they are being whisked away from their desk for a surprise vacation in just a few hours. They would even love to have one of those makeover shows show up at their house with a film crew and learn they're getting a whole new wardrobe.

Surprises feel thrilling to them. Like how some people feel when a roller-coaster ride they thought was over suddenly takes off again and starts doing upside-down loops. They throw their hands in the air and embrace the thrill of the unknown. They call that fun.

I don't.

I can usually manage my dislike of surprises in all the situations I mentioned. My friends know not to throw me a surprise party. After the initial shock and resistance to the unplanned and unexpected, a surprise vacation or a new wardrobe could be nice. I might even be able to stomach a roller coaster, if I can thoroughly check it out and know its patterned route before I agree to ride it.

But life is different.

Life twists and turns and throws loops into places we think will be flat and smooth. Because that's what life does. Sometimes it just catches us off guard.

At the end of the day, I guess that's why I don't like to be surprised. Getting caught off guard makes me feel exposed, afraid, and put on the spot before I've had any time to think through my response.

But slowly, I'm learning it's not all bad to be surprised.

That vulnerable place reminds us we have needs beyond what we can manage. Feeling a little exposed and afraid reminds us we need God. Desperately. Completely.

And in that gap between what we think we can manage on our own and what we can't is right where faith has the opportunity to grow deep roots. Roots that dig down into the hope and joy and peace only God can offer.

I'm challenging myself to remember my faith doesn't just need to grow big—it needs to grow deep (Jeremiah 17:7–8).

How do we get deep roots? We grow deep spiritual roots the same way a tree grows deep physical roots. The roots of a tree will never go through the pain and effort of digging deeper until there isn't enough water from the surface to satisfy it. There's water to be found in the deeper places. But the gift of going through the hardship to get to the deeper water is that deeper roots can help the tree withstand thrashing winds from bigger storms when they come.

And they will come. A tree with shallow roots is in great danger of being knocked down and taken out.

We are much the same. Shallow seeking will produce shallow believing and leave us vulnerable to falling. But deep seeking will produce deep believing and equip us to stand firm, no matter what may catch us off guard.

Deep roots keep us secure in God's love when fear comes.

Deep roots anchor us with the truth that God is in control when unexpected hardships surround us like unruly winds.

Deep roots hold us steady in God's peace during the storm that didn't show up on the radar.

Deep roots find nourishment in God's grace when the surface gets awfully dry.

Deep roots propel us to grow stronger in our faith in God that we might not otherwise be desperate enough to do.

I'm learning not to be so afraid of what might be around the next corner, even if it does catch me off guard. I close my eyes and whisper to the Lord, "Deeper still." And with that, I may not be completely ready, but I can be much more *steady* with each next step.

My faith doesn't just need to grow big—it needs to grow deep.

EVENING

Steady steps. That's how I want to walk through everything I face. *Steady* means "firmly fixed, supported, or balanced; not shaking or moving."[1] The definition of *unsteady* is "liable to fall or shake; not steady in position."[2]

I find these definitions to be fascinating. If I want to take steady steps, then I need to be fixed, supported, or balanced. It's comforting to me to know that God is always steady—nothing catches God off guard. He is never surprised. He's never thrown off balance. Therefore, the more I listen to Him and stay with Him, the more I am fixed, supported, and balanced alongside Him.

Tonight, I want you to think about these questions:

Where am I tempted to run ahead of God?
Where am I tempted to drag my feet and lag behind God?
Where am I getting it right and staying in step with God?
What feels steady in my life?
What feels like an unsteady place in my life where I'm more liable to fall or shake?

I believe praying through these questions will help us be more mindful about where we are really standing with God and where we may not be. Remaining steady through all of life's unexpected ups and downs is really only possible when we are remaining right alongside God in the process. The world will always try to make big promises about what will make us feel better. But it's only when we are walking in obedience to God that we will genuinely heal better and be made more and more steady.

SOMETHING TO RELEASE BACK TO GOD FROM TODAY:

_____

_____

A PRAYER TO RECEIVE BEFORE TOMORROW:

Lord, I'm so thankful You're in control and You always have a plan. More than I dislike being caught off guard, I love You and I trust You. Help my roots grow deep as I open my hands and my heart in surrender to You. Thank You for the healing perspectives You are showing me in the pages of this book. In Jesus' name, amen.

DAY 41

We Can't
Please
All the
People All the Time . . . and That's Okay

Am I now trying to win the approval of human beings, or of God? Or am I trying to please people? If I were still trying to please people, I would not be a servant of Christ.

GALATIANS 1:10

MORNING

Throughout the pages of this book, we've processed where we might consider drawing some healthy boundaries in our relationships. While it can be overwhelming, I have found boundaries to be essential in pursuing healing, emotional maturity, and healthy relationships.

But more than that, boundaries aren't just a good idea; they're a God idea.

While I can encourage you to draw healthy boundaries, I wouldn't be a good friend to you if I didn't also warn you of some obstacles you will more than likely run into as you try to make these necessary changes. One of those obstacles I've had to acknowledge (and imperfectly overcome) is people pleasing.

You see, somewhere along the way, I picked up a mindset that people's opinions define who I am. This made me the perfect candidate to resist boundary setting and view any kind of boundaries as unkind. In an effort to be incredibly honest with you, sometimes I still find myself working really hard to untangle myself from this mindset.

I don't know where you are today, but maybe you're trying to untangle yourself out of it too.

The problem is that if we let other people's opinions define who we are, we will be desperate to try to control people's perceptions of us. We will spend our lives managing opinions to be always favorable toward us so we can feel good about ourselves. But think about the tragic reality of this—being too concerned with gaining the approval of others can give us divided hearts with God. Ouch.

It's impossible to please all the people all the time. We know this. Until we forget—especially with people whose opinions affect us. So, when we disappoint people, think differently than they do, don't do what they think we should do, or try to draw boundaries they don't agree with, then others might think poorly of us. And if they think poorly of us, we fear it will be impossible to feel good about ourselves.

I think this hits at the core fear around setting boundaries. If I set a boundary, people will no longer see me as I want them to see me. They will no longer know me as I want them to know me. They will no longer believe the best about me, and there's something inside me that really wants them to believe the best about me.

When we try to set boundaries and people respond with statements that don't accurately portray who we are, it can feel as if we're being absolutely misunderstood and wrongly labeled. Then to fight against that negative label being put on us, we all too often drop the boundary. We would rather suffer through the other person's boundary violations than deal with that person judging us wrongly.

Ugh. Hello, me. Hello, you?

It is so very important that we are aware of feelings and mindsets like this that can make us vulnerable to not establishing wise boundaries in our relationships. If we are afraid that people will think poorly of us, potentially abandon us, or try to make us feel crazy for taking a step toward making the relationship healthy, chances are even higher that, without wise boundaries, they will eventually do all three of these things to us. (Dear me: read that last sentence one more time . . . maybe ten more times.)

With all this said, before you really start your day, knock out your to-do list, and conquer all the things, I want to leave you with these simple words I first wrote in my journal and then put in my book *Uninvited* years ago: God's love is not based on us; it's simply placed on us. And it's from this place that we should live . . . loved.

Do I want to be loved by others? Of course I do. Do I want to fear that another person's love for me is based on me always making that person happy? Absolutely not. Love should be what draws us together, not what tears us apart.

God's love is not based on us; it's simply placed on us.

And it's from this place we should live . . . loved.

EVENING

When I feel misunderstood in my boundaries, I cling to these good verses from Colossians 1:10–11: "So that you may live a life worthy of the Lord and please him in every way: bearing fruit in every good work, growing in the knowledge of God, being strengthened with all power according to his glorious might so that you may have great endurance and patience."

I want to keep myself in the place of living a life worthy of the Lord. I want to please Him. I want to bear fruit. I want to grow and be strengthened by God. I want to have endurance and patience. That's what prompts me to ask myself as I'm considering a boundary I may need to put in place, *Am I more or less likely to live out these verses with this boundary?*

I want us to really consider this before we go to sleep tonight. As you reflect on any necessary changes you may need to make in your own life, first pray and ask God to help you receive from Him who you really are. He created you and made you in His very own image. If you capture an image of His goodness, you'll find some part of you there.

As you consider releasing the desire to give in to people-please tonight, remember how loved you are. The more full of God's love you are, the less tempted you'll be to settle for others' scraps of love. What a freeing way to live . . . loved.

SOMETHING TO RELEASE BACK TO GOD FROM TODAY:

_____

_____

A PRAYER TO RECEIVE BEFORE TOMORROW:

Jesus, thank You for being such a safe place for me to return to when I'm struggling. When I'm tempted to look to others for validation and acceptance, please remind me to look up at You. I pray that the Holy Spirit would help me take inventory of my own life, understand the limitations of my capacity, and consider any potential boundaries I need to implement in my relationships. In Jesus' name, amen.

DAY **42**

Who I Am Doesn't
Feel Good Enough

> "I am the Lord's servant," Mary answered.
> "May your word to me be fulfilled."
>
> LUKE 1:38

MORNING

Do you ever struggle with feeling like maybe God should have picked someone else to fulfill your roles? As a mom, a business owner, leader, employee, neighbor, or friend?

I remember a time when I begged God to make me just like the super-organized mom I heard speak at a parenting seminar. I mentally listed what I discerned must be her secret to success and set about to imitate her. But it didn't take long before I was absolutely miserable. I mentally beat myself up for not having what it obviously took to be a great mom. What was wrong with me?

Then one day in Bible study, I read the story of Mary, the teenage mother of Jesus. My heart beat fast as I realized she didn't meet the standard of Supermom that I'd set for myself.

Somehow, just as she was, God chose young Mary to be Jesus' mother. And the only qualification she seemed to have was her willingness. We see her trust in God's plan revealed Luke 1:38: "'I am the Lord's servant,' Mary answered. 'May your word to me be fulfilled.'"

Mary could have easily rattled off a list of the reasons she should be passed over for such an incredible privilege.

Too young.
Too poor.
Too inexperienced.

Just a simple girl from a simple town. Yet we find the angel Gabriel standing before her in Luke 1, proclaiming she had been chosen. That she, Mary, was the blessed and highly favored vessel God wanted to use to bring forth His one and only Son, Jesus. The Messiah (Luke 1:30–33).

Mary had only one question: "'How will this be,' Mary asked the angel, 'since I am a virgin?'" (Luke 1:34).

Gabriel graciously answered, explaining to Mary that the Holy Spirit would come upon her, and the power of the Most High would overshadow her. The angel told her about the miraculous pregnancy of her much-older cousin Elizabeth, and he reminded Mary that what seemed impossible to her was absolutely possible with God (Luke 1:35–37).

I confess I am humbled and amazed by Mary's question. All she wanted to know was how the pregnancy was going to be physically possible.

She didn't ask any of the questions I might have been tempted to ask, like, "Are you sure you have the right person? Don't you know how unqualified I am? Have you considered asking one of the women just down the street? Surely any one of them would be a better choice than me."

It's so easy to look around and think there are plenty of other people more qualified than we are, isn't it? All God wanted from Mary was her willingness. And He let me know that day in Bible study it was all He wanted from me too. He had already given me the exact qualities He knew my kids would need in a mother. I just needed to lift up my willingness to Him daily and let Him help me be the best version of me.

Maybe you aren't feeling very qualified today. Maybe you feel like God should pass over you and pick someone else for the assignments He's placed before you. If that's you, I want you to know this—God loves to take ordinary people and do extraordinary things in them, through them, and with them.

God's not waiting on you to impress Him. He simply wants you to say yes to Him.

Let's stop offering God our excuses and lists of why He can't work in us and through us. As long as we have breath in our lungs, God is still working in us. God is still helping us heal. The key to experiencing healing today is not wishing we were someone else but instead laying down our measuring sticks of perfection and humbly bowing our heads as we offer Him our willingness today.

Yes, Lord. I'm Yours. All of me. All for You.

A statement to remember as I walk into today:

God's not waiting on you to impress Him. He simply wants you to say yes to Him.

EVENING

I thought raising kids was a job that lasted around twenty years, then I'd cross a glorious finish line and just be friends with these glorious humans now fully grown. But now I'm realizing fully grown doesn't always mean fully ready to face the pitfalls of living in an imperfect and sometimes brutal world. I don't say this to discourage you if you have younger kids, but having kids in their twenties and thirties has proven to be the most challenging phase of my motherhood journey.

A big reason is I've had to learn how to shift my mothering. My kids are adults living in their own houses, having their own kids, and paying their own bills. My influence should guide them when they ask me for help—not automatically demand they do things my way. This is hard! Sometimes I get it right, and sometimes I totally bomb. But I'm willing to make the necessary shifts from what was appropriate when they were ten years old to what's more reasonable now that they are grown. I can make suggestions but not inappropriate demands. I can guide them but not control them. I can help them but not enable them. I can hurt when they hurt but not own their issues as if they are mine to fix.

This shift is good to think about whether you're mothering kids or mentoring kids. Our goal shouldn't just be to raise children. We want to raise capable adults whom we love and release.

Let's pray tonight that God would show us how to invite Him in to our assignments, knowing even when we don't feel good enough, His strength compensates for every weakness.

SOMETHING TO RELEASE BACK TO GOD FROM TODAY:

_____

_____

A PRAYER TO RECEIVE BEFORE TOMORROW:

God, sometimes I feel unqualified and unable to complete the assignments You have put in front of me. Today, I'm so thankful for the strength and support You provide. Thank You for choosing me and loving me enough not only to save me but also to give me purpose. I'm looking for opportunities to say yes to this week. In Jesus' name, amen.

DAY

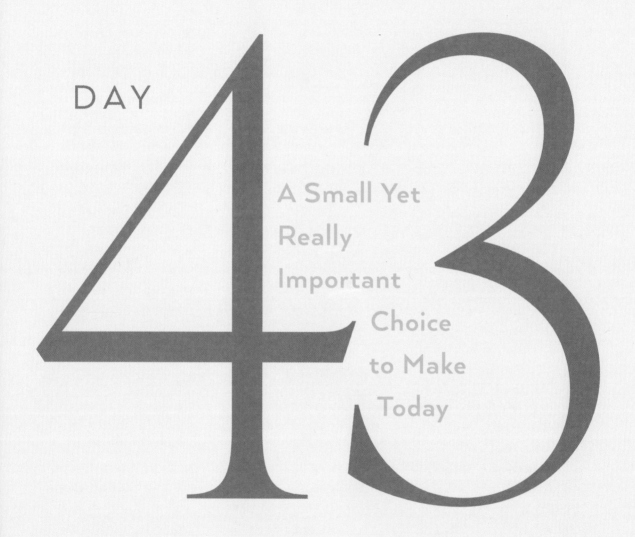

43

A Small Yet
Really
Important
Choice
to Make
Today

> "Whoever can be trusted with very little can also be trusted with much."
>
> LUKE 16:10

MORNING

We have a choice today.

We can look out and see the unlimited, abundant opportunities God has placed before us. To create. To serve. To love. To heal. To accomplish.

Or we can stare at the opportunity another person may be stepping into right now and get entangled in the Enemy's lie that everything is in scarce supply. Scarce opportunities. Scarce possibilities.

Yesterday we talked about Mary and wondered how she might have felt about her assignment to be the mother of Jesus. But beyond having a marked moment with God, deciding we want to be used by Him, I also want us to be careful not to see a sister next to us as a threat to our own stories.

When this happens, we start to see her progress as threatening to our slower process. We start to see her accomplishments as a threat to our opportunities. We can start to push away from people we should be cheering for because we're stuck staring and comparing ourselves.

I pray today that whatever God is asking of us, we will say yes with willing hearts, trusting His timing, and embracing what He's asking *us* to do today:

- that phone call He's been prompting us to make
- that counseling session He's been reminding us to reschedule
- that neighbor who we know would love to spend some quality time with us
- that step of forgiveness He's inviting us to take with another person

Whatever it is, big or small, it will be more significant than what we might ever discern beforehand. Whatever God leads us to, He will lead us through. But we often get stuck by being disobedient to a step He's prompted us to take.

God might take you on unlikely paths through quiet seasons where you wonder if you heard Him wrong. I know how disillusioning this can feel.

How come that other woman seems to be fast-tracked in her healing and is now helping others, while my progress feels much slower? So small. So unnoticed.

She is—and you are—significant to Him.

How can I see God turn my pain into a purposeful ministry when after preparing my Bible study lesson for weeks, only three women showed up?

Those three women are so very significant to Him.

How can all the time it takes to go to counseling and dig into the past be part of a grand plan to move forward?

Your healing is significant to Him.

The moment when you realize that every step you take is significant to God, you'll be more likely to obey Him rather than resist Him. That will be the moment you see that life is not about the destination; it's about staying in alignment with God's heart.

Protect that alignment with the fiercest passion and every bit of fight you have in you. Being with Jesus is the high calling. Everything else is just homework.

And the journey seems to be the most joyful when we cheer on one another together.

A statement to remember as I walk into today:

Life is not about the destination; it's about staying in alignment with God's heart.

EVENING

Big steps of healing are always made up of many small, wise decisions. Here are some examples to consider:

- Choose some new, healthy habits. The time you no longer waste trying to fix another person can now be invested into your own journey toward health and healing.
- Lead your thought life. Instead of spending countless hours obsessing over what happened, set a timer and give yourself five minutes to focus on the hard stuff. Then lead your thoughts in a different direction. There are many other wonderful things to think through and dream about.
- Reach out and plan to do something fun with a friend. Sadness often makes us want to isolate. Instead of shutting others out of your life, take small steps to invite them in.
- Don't assume everything is better for everyone else. Our issues can feel all-consuming. But

when others say they are praying for you, in addition to inviting them into your requests, ask them how they are doing, too, and how you can pray for them.

- Resist the temptation to write scripts in your head based on what the person who hurt you might be saying. Find a counselor to help you process your pain based on facts and not assumptions.

SOMETHING TO RELEASE BACK TO GOD FROM TODAY:

_____

_____

A PRAYER TO RECEIVE BEFORE TOMORROW:

Heavenly Father, it's so easy to overlook the small things—the small decisions, the small ways You're moving in my life, the small steps of progress I've experienced in my healing journey. Give me eyes to see You move in the big and small. I know it all matters to You. In Jesus' name, amen.

DAY

44

Consider the
Source

The tongue of the wise adorns knowledge, but
the mouth of the fool gushes folly.
PROVERBS 15:2

MORNING

It was one of those voice mails that left me rubbing my head wondering, *What do I do with all she just said?* I was blindsided by the criticism and felt this would be the perfect time to find a hole and crawl into it.

Criticism hurts. No matter who you are, how many people are encouraging you, and how happy you felt before you got that call or that email or that comment on social media.

When we're trying to keep our hearts swept clean, pursue Jesus, read His Word, and take steps of healing every single day, we have a choice in *these* things. We can stay disciplined in these things. But criticism is different. We can be trying our best to do the right things, and criticism still shows up on our front doorstep completely unsolicited and usually at the worst time.

In these moments, I wish I had an escape route. But I don't.

However, I do have a perspective shift that has helped me, and I want to encourage you with it today: harsh and unnecessary criticism says a lot more about that person's insecurities than our inadequacies.

This isn't to puff ourselves up in pride and shame the other person. No, it's a posture of humility that allows me to maintain a compassionate heart when criticisms are thrown at me. Rather than reacting out of defensiveness and emotion, I can consider the source of this criticism and discern if this person is offering this to help me or is throwing this at me with the intent to hurt me.

If there's some truth to the criticism, we should consider a course correction. However, if the criticism is destructive and hurtful, we must remember the words of Proverbs 15:2: "The mouth of the fool gushes folly." The definition of *folly* is a "lack of understanding or sense."[1]

Again, this verse isn't meant to weaponize and label the one criticizing us as a fool. But the criticism may reveal there is a lack of understanding driving what the person said. My counselor, Jim Cress, often says, "People are down on what they are not up on."

As I mentioned in Day 16, Jim also reminds me to "Get curious, not furious." Sometimes asking questions instead of immediately trying to defend myself helps me stay more calm. Questions like, "Would you help me understand why this is bothering you so much?" or "Thank you for caring about me enough to bring this to my attention. What are you hoping I do with this information?"

We might not feel like being calm at first. But I'm learning that staying calm is as much of a gift to myself as it is to the one criticizing me. We can't fix whatever hurt caused this person to lash out. But we can decide to stay calm and not multiply the hurt with more criticism in return. Proverbs 15:1 instructs, "A gentle answer turns away wrath, but a harsh word stirs up anger."

Criticism in any form hurts because it sticks. We are much more likely to remember one critical comment than a hundred positive comments. Why is this? An article published by CBS News provided some fascinating insight on this: "And that kind of pain [criticism] is hard to shake for any of us. So why are unpleasant things so unforgettable? Scientists call it negativity bias. The theory is that bad news makes a much bigger impact on our brains."[2] The article goes on to say that it's been this way since our lives depended on being able to remember, above all, what could kill us, as means for survival.

Our brains want to know we are safe, we aren't being threatened, and we can move forward in confidence. If I remember this, I am much more likely to understand some of the emotional charge that happens when criticism comes my way. I will better be able to manage my reaction if I lead my brain with thoughts like, *This is one person's opinion, but it isn't the entire world's opinion. If there is something helpful in what they are saying, then I can take that and release the rest. I'm safe, and I can move forward.*

While we can't choose what comes at us, we can choose not to compound it by adding our poor reactions into the mix. We can respond with a gentle, God-honoring response or at least open up needed dialogue. And certainly, we cannot let this hurt propel us to criticize them and cause more and more hurt.

Let's determine today that unnecessarily harsh criticism ends with us.

A statement to remember as I walk into today:

Harsh and unnecessary criticism says a lot more about that person's insecurities than our inadequacies.

EVENING

While the words of criticism sting, there are other powerful, beneficial ways we can use our words. Before we go to sleep tonight, let's look at some verses containing instructional wisdom for how to use our words in a God-honoring way:

- "Do not let any unwholesome talk come out of your mouths, but only what is helpful for building others up according to their needs, that it may benefit those who listen" (Ephesians 4:29).
- "The words of the reckless pierce like swords, but the tongue of the wise brings healing" (Proverbs 12:18).
- "Gracious words are a honeycomb, sweet to the soul and healing to the bones" (Proverbs 16:24).
- "May these words of my mouth and this meditation of my heart be pleasing in your sight, Lord, my Rock and my Redeemer" (Psalm 19:14).

Our words are a direct reflection of our hearts. And your heart is much too beautiful of a place to be filled with harsh, critical, demanding, or unhealed perspectives.

As our hearts are healing, let's make sure our words are focused on healing and not hurting. "For the mouth speaks what the heart is full of" (Luke 6:45).

SOMETHING TO RELEASE BACK TO GOD FROM TODAY:

_____

_____

A PRAYER TO RECEIVE BEFORE TOMORROW:

God, criticisms can cut my heart so deeply. Heal my heart of any past critical scripts I'm still holding on to. Help me release any hurtful accusations or comments and instead walk in the identity You've given me today. I love You, Lord. In Jesus' name, amen.

DAY 45

Encouragement for a Grieving Heart

> ## "O death, where is your victory? O death, where is your sting?"
> ### 1 CORINTHIANS 15:55 ESV

MORNING

Losing someone you love can cut into your heart so viciously that it forever redefines who you are and how you think. It's what I call deep grief.

I know some of you may find yourselves facing this kind of pain right now.

It strains against everything you've ever believed. So much so, you wonder how the promises that seemed so real on those thin Bible pages yesterday could possibly stand up under the weight of this enormous sadness today.

This is part of what makes talking about death so difficult. The mere mention of death and dying can stir up a tremendous amount of unresolved grief.

I remember standing at the side of a casket too small to accept. Pink roses were draped everywhere. My heart was stunned and shattered. There are still certain dates on the calendar that can trigger a flood of questions and pain surrounding the tragic loss of my baby sister. I imagine you have days like that too.

But it's not just grief that makes it hard. There can also be a lot of fear. Fear of other loved ones dying. Fear of our own death. Fear of what the process of dying might be like for us. It can all feel so overwhelming and paralyzing.

How thankful I am that Scripture holds powerful truths we can remember when the fear of dying tries to keep us from truly living. We can feel afraid, but we don't have to live afraid.

We are taught early on as Christians that "the wages of sin is death" (Romans 6:23 ESV) and that Jesus came to pay that price for us. Hebrews 2:17 says He came "to make propitiation for the sins of the people" (ESV). The definition of the Greek word used here for "propitiation," *hilaskomai*, means both "to make atonement" and "to show mercy."[1]

I love how we see the mercy of Jesus on display in Hebrews 2:14–15: "Since the children have flesh and blood, he too shared in their humanity so that by his death he might break the power of him who holds the power of death—that is, the devil—and free those who all their lives were held in slavery by their fear of death."

These words feel so very personal.

What grace and kindness, Jesus would come to free us both from the power of death and the fear of it.

Donald Guthrie stated in his commentary on Hebrews that it seems "paradoxical that Christ used death as a means of destroying the maliciousness of death."[2] But because death had become a reality for us as a result of sin, only the offering of Jesus' sinless life could reverse this curse (Romans 5:12–17).

Through His death, Jesus defeated death for us. And His resurrected body allows us now to declare, "O death, where is your victory? O death, where is your sting?" (1 Corinthians 15:55 ESV).

This doesn't mean our hearts won't ever experience deep grief or feel the pain of loss this side of eternity. Even if you stripped a lethally poisonous scorpion of its venom, its sting would still hurt. But the scorpion's strike would no longer hold the power to end your life. This is what Jesus has done. He has removed the fatality of death's sting. He has given us the victory (1 Corinthians 15:57).

For those who believe in Jesus Christ as Lord of their lives, death isn't the end. It's another beginning. Death is but a passageway at God's designated time for us finally to escape this broken world full of imperfections and be welcomed to the perfect, eternal home we've been longing for our entire lives (Revelation 21:4).

I know how incredibly hard all this can be. But let's hold on to the sweet knowledge that Jesus has already gone before us. We don't have to be afraid.

And if you're struggling with the piercing pain of deep grief right now?

Give yourself grace to face this. Even when we know without a doubt that someday we will see our loved one again, the reality of deep grief is that it takes time. It takes prayer. It takes wading through an ocean of tears, only to discover one day that the sun is still shining.

Keep clinging to the knowledge that even in our grief, God is near and every one of His promises is true.

A statement to remember as I walk into today:

Even in our grief, God is near and every one of His promises is true.

EVENING

In this world, loss makes us grieve, as it should. But this heartbreak that can seem so final still contains hope. At the very same time we grieve a loss, we gain more and more awareness of an eternal perspective. Grieving is such a deep work and a long process, it feels like we might not survive it. But eventually we do. And even though we still may never agree on this side of eternity that the trade God gave us is worth what we've lost, we hold on to hope by trusting God's promise that this world is like vapor, but eternity is forever (James 4:14). So though we cry, we can place this loss in God's hands.

Everything lost that we place in the hands of God isn't a forever loss.

Martin Luther said, "I have held many things in my hands, and I have lost them all; but whatever I have placed in God's hands, that I still possess."[3]

God took Adam's bone. He gave him back the gift of a woman. God took Abraham from his family's land. He gave him back a promised land and descendants as numerous as the stars in the sky (Genesis 26:4). God took Jesus through a brutal crucifixion. He gave back salvation for the world. Not everything that's been taken from us was by the hand of God. But when I mentally place each and every loss in His hands, it can be redeemed. Loss is never the end of the story.

Here's the sobering truth: no human gets through life without being deeply, deeply hurt at some point. Grief finds all of us. As we process our own grief, I pray we also cultivate soft hearts that grow attentive and tender toward other people in their grief.

We have a beautiful invitation for tonight—to bring it all into the hands of Jesus. He is with you in your grief, sweet friend. Remember the words of Psalm 34:18, "The LORD is close to the brokenhearted and saves those who are crushed in spirit."

SOMETHING TO RELEASE BACK TO GOD FROM TODAY:

_____

_____

A PRAYER TO RECEIVE BEFORE TOMORROW:

Oh Lord, You are close to me in my grief. I don't want to let the heartbreak I've experienced lead to going through the motions in my relationship with You or relationship with others. Show me who might be a trusted friend I can confide in during this difficult time. This may be a hard time, but I'm also declaring it a holy time marked by closeness with You. In Jesus' name, amen.

DAY 46

It All Comes Down to Choice

> The seed that fell among thorns stands for those who hear, but as they go on their way they are choked by life's worries, riches and pleasures, and they do not mature.
>
> LUKE 8:14

MORNING

For most of us, life hasn't been a bed of roses.

What an odd statement. It's supposed to mean that I haven't lived a life without snags and hurt. However, think of an actual bed of roses. Doesn't it have both thorns and flowers?

My aunt grew roses for years. She's the one I lived with for almost a year when I was in middle school and my family was falling apart. I remember her telling me not to run through her rose garden. After all, she had a lot of land that unfolded in wide open fields. I could run there.

But I didn't want to.

I only wanted to run through the rose garden. I wanted to spread my arms wide open and run between the rows, brushing my fingertips across all the velvety blooms. I wanted some of the blooms to burst and shower petals all around. Then I could gather the petals and spread them along my path.

I wanted my world to be soft, pink, and lovely. I didn't want to think about my dad leaving our family. My heart couldn't process how he not only didn't live with us anymore, but he was also slowly pulling back from participating in our lives altogether.

So I took a running start with my arms outstretched, only to be shocked with searing pain within the first few steps.

Thorns. Big, mean, vicious thorns. Thorns that ripped my flesh and released the flood of tears I'd been so determined to hold back. Suddenly, I hated that bush. I wanted to chop it down and beat it into the ground. But I couldn't do it. I couldn't bring myself to destroy something that produced such beauty.

I stood back from the source of my pain and wondered, *Should I call it a bush of thorns or a bush of flowers?* Really, it could go either way.

Suddenly I wasn't just staring at a bush. I was staring at my life. My life. Such a bed of roses.

Would I see the hurt, or would I see the beauty?

Luke 8:14 says, "The seed that fell among thorns stands for those who hear, but as they go on their way they are choked by life's worries, riches and pleasures, and they do not mature." The seed being referred to here is the Word of God. Isn't it interesting that people who are choked by life's circumstances and never mature are referred to as having thorns in the soil of their soul?

Yes, sometimes life hands us thorns, but we have the choice to park our minds on the thorn or on the beauty it can eventually produce in us if only we'll cling tightly to God's Word. How people think is how they will eventually become.

If we dwell on the negative in life, we'll become negative, and God's Word will have a hard time taking root in our souls. If, however, we acknowledge the negative but choose instead to look for the good that can come from it, God's Word will take root in our souls and produce a lush crop of beauty.

It all comes down to our choice. That day in my aunt's garden, I chose to be aware of the thorns but park my mind on the beautiful roses.

And over the years, I have come to the place where I realize I can focus on the hurt my dad's absence caused, or I can choose to focus on other things in my life. Beautiful things. Focusing on beauty isn't to deny the pain. It's just refusing to let it steal anything else from me.

It's been more than thirty years since I've seen my biological dad. That's hard on a girl's heart. But where he fell so short, God has filled in many gaps. I don't have to be the child of a broken parent the rest of my life; I can be a child of God. Loved. Truly loved.

A statement to remember as I walk into today:

Focusing on beauty isn't to deny the pain. It's just refusing to let it steal anything else from us.

EVENING

The happiest people aren't the ones whose lives are perfect. The happiest people are the ones who are most capable of keeping the imperfections in perspective. Just because some things are hard doesn't mean everything is hard.

I'm still learning this lesson myself.

There is no such thing as a perfect day. A perfect week. A perfect life. A perfect home. A perfect family.

The more we resist this reality, the less we'll enjoy the sweet and special moments of our life. Because here's a little-known secret about imperfections: what makes things most beautiful, most memorable, and most notable are those unexpected gifts wrapped in imperfections.

Imperfections help others uncross their arms, relax, and giggle. We can easily focus on something that didn't go "right" and let that ruin a moment, or we can laugh it off and say to ourselves, "This will be a great story one day."

Simply put, if you bring the happy, your life will be beautiful.

Not perfect, but beautiful.

Embrace the unexpected. Smile at the crazy. Laugh at the unplanned. And relax. Make the intentional decision right now that tomorrow, if you bring the happy, your day will be beautiful.

SOMETHING TO RELEASE BACK TO GOD FROM TODAY:

_____

_____

A PRAYER TO RECEIVE BEFORE TOMORROW:

Dear Lord, it can be really hard to focus on the petals rather than the thorns of life. But I want the soil of my soul to be healthy and ready to receive Your Word. Will You produce beauty in my life despite the thorns that have hurt me? In Jesus' name, amen.

DAY 47

Three Steps
to Overcome
Anxious
Thoughts

> Peace I leave with you; my peace I give you. I do not give to you as the world gives. Do not let your hearts be troubled and do not be afraid.
>
> JOHN 14:27

MORNING

Anxiety. Not one of us is completely immune to heart-stabbing, pulse-racing anxious feelings.

Most of us have had a personal struggle with this peace stealer.

I'm so thankful God spoke into this struggle in the Bible. It reminds us that God doesn't want our lives to be constantly hijacked by anxiety. He doesn't want us walking through our days or lying in our beds at night tormented by anxious thoughts. He also doesn't want us making decisions from a place of fear and missing out on seeing the good things He has for us.

Even Jesus Himself spoke to this topic when He told us in John 14:27 that He left us with peace. *Peace.* Not worry. Not fear. Not anxiety.

Make no mistake, sweet friends, the Enemy wants us to feel hopeless. He wants us to live enslaved to our worries and fears. But God wants us to know that we don't have to let anxiety rob us of our peace, our hope, or our joy another single day.

Instead of allowing anxious thoughts to wreak havoc in our hearts and minds, let's try these three steps:

1. *Pray honestly.* Prayer connects our overwhelming anxiety to God's overcoming power. God can help us redirect our hearts and minds away from anxious thoughts and onto truths and safe assurances found in Him. We have full permission to pour out our hearts to Him honestly. We can bring every fear, every request, every need to Him without hesitation or apology (1 Peter 5:7). When we do, we'll find that prayer and peace walk hand in hand.
2. *Read God's truths.* We can intentionally think on truth by seeking out scriptures that speak to the issues we are facing. When we tuck God's truth into our hearts, we are arming ourselves with the most powerful tool available—His Word! (Hebrews 4:12).
3. *Verbalize trust in Him.* We can quote the scriptures we've memorized throughout our day. There is tremendous power in quoting a verse slowly and intentionally—claiming the truths contained within and verbalizing our belief in God out loud.

I'm convinced the more we draw near to God in prayer and the more we fill our minds with His Word, the more crowded out our fears and anxieties will become.

Prayer connects our overwhelming anxiety to God's overcoming power.

EVENING

There's a popular Bible passage people like to quote about anxiety, found in Philippians 4:6–7: "Do not be anxious about anything, but in every situation, by prayer and petition, with thanksgiving, present your requests to God. And the peace of God, which transcends all understanding, will guard your hearts and your minds in Christ Jesus."

I love these verses. I've taught my kids these verses. And as I've spent time studying it, I've noticed something interesting—the four very powerful words in the verse right before it. Philippians 4:5 ends with, "The Lord is near." And because the Lord is near, we don't have to be anxious. We have the assurance of His soothing presence.

When I put this verse in context and see how God promises to be with me and those I love, this verse takes on a whole new meaning for me.

It's His presence plus His promise that chases away our anxious thoughts.

SOMETHING TO RELEASE BACK TO GOD FROM TODAY:

_____

_____

A PRAYER TO RECEIVE BEFORE TOMORROW:

Father God, thank You for the tender ways You offer to help me when my heart feels anxious and fearful. Instead of shaming me for my feelings, You offer to sit with me in the midst of them. Instead of expecting me to pull myself together, You offer me Your words that hold me together and bring me peace. You are such a good and gracious Father. One I know I can trust and call on, at all times. In Jesus' name, amen.

DAY

48

The Power
to Live
Out
Scripture Even When It Feels Impossible

MORNING

I know what it feels like to have been hurt so deeply that living out the commands of Scripture to forgive seems too cruel even to consider.

How can I offer forgiveness as Colossians 3:13 commands ("Bear with each other and forgive one another if any of you has a grievance against someone. Forgive as the Lord forgave you.") when someone has wounded me to the point where I fear I'll never feel normal again? And how can I be expected to be a woman of grace and compassion as Ephesians 4:32 asks of me when the pain seems never-ending and the one who hurt me acts like it's no big deal?

These are questions pulsing not just with pain and loss but also with a grief so deep it can feel maddening to think Scripture should apply in these circumstances.

And this is exactly when I must remember that truth proclaimed and lived out is a fiercely accurate weapon against evil. Truth says I have an Enemy, but it's not the person whose choices have caused me great pain.

Yes, people have a choice to sin against us or not. And certainly, when we are hurt, the person hurting us willingly played into the Enemy's plan. But it helps me to remember what Paul taught in Ephesians 6:10–13—that people aren't my real Enemy. The devil is real and on an all-out assault against all things good. He hates the word *together*. And he intentionally schemes and works against relationships. But we are told in Scripture that we can take a stand against the schemes of the Enemy.

Ephesians 6:11 reminds us we need to "Put on the whole armor of God, that you may be able to stand against the schemes of the devil" (ESV).

The phrase "may be able" (which is translated "can" in the NIV) is *dynasthai* in the original Greek form, meaning "I am powerful—I have the power."[1] We may feel powerless when the Enemy stirs up trouble among us, but we aren't. The secret is to be aware of this. And it's knowing where that power comes from.

When Paul commanded us in Ephesians 6:10 to "be strong," it can be interpreted in the original Greek in the passive voice. Paul was saying we should be "made strong, or be strengthened." There is tremendous freedom to be found in this subtle difference. God isn't calling us to find a power within ourselves to overcome the battles we face. The reason we can "be strong in the Lord and in the strength of his might" (Ephesians 6:10 ESV) is that the very same power of God that raised Christ from the dead through the Spirit lives in us (Ephesians 1:19–21).

The power is not in question. But our awareness of it often rises and falls on our willingness to do what God's Word says to do in times of conflict. This doesn't mean we overlook offenses that should be addressed. It doesn't mean we tolerate destructive behaviors and allow those who have hurt us free access to keep hurting us. No, but it does mean we chose to live out God's Word no matter what response is needed in each situation we face.

We won't get this right all the time. But focusing on God's Word will develop a bent toward forgiveness and away from bitterness. Remember, it's often when we don't want to live out God's Word with another person that doing what God says is an epic defeat of the Enemy. Hurt feelings don't often want to cooperate with holy instructions. But there is nothing more powerful than a person living what God's Word teaches.

A statement to remember as I walk into today:

Hurt feelings don't often want to cooperate with holy instructions.

EVENING

If no one else in this world has been kind enough to say this, I will. I'm so, so sorry for all that's happened to you.

I'm so sorry for the unfair and cruel things you may be facing.

But friend, before you go to sleep tonight, let's settle this truth deep in our spirits: God's Word is good, and it's for our good. He has not left us powerless to live it out. No matter what we're going through, let's resolve to stay in step with God and stay committed to reading His Word and living out its instructions. Let's not fall asleep tonight once again obsessing over all the wrongs done to us lately. Let's receive God's truth and rest in the peace and perspectives that lead us toward healing tonight.

SOMETHING TO RELEASE BACK TO GOD FROM TODAY:

_____

_____

A PRAYER TO RECEIVE BEFORE TOMORROW:

Father God, I'm so thankful You haven't left me unprepared for the battles I face. I have Your Word to guide me, Your Spirit deep inside me, and Your armor to protect me. Help me remember who my real Enemy is. And give me the strength and the wisdom to live in obedience to You, no matter what my feelings might say. In Jesus' name, amen.

DAY 49

Moving On
When That
Relationship
Doesn't

> ### If possible, so far as it depends on
> ### you, live peaceably with all.
>
> ROMANS 12:18 ESV

MORNING

I'm strong. I'm long-suffering. I'm loyal to a fault. My love is strong enough to withstand it all. I don't give up. I don't walk away. I won't walk away.

Some of the best parts of me don't seem to line up with someone who reaches a place in a relationship where it's no longer sustainable and can't go on. Romans 12:18 has tripped me up sometimes when it says, "If possible, so far as it depends on you, live peaceably with all" (ESV). But I recently realized that Paul intentionally used the phrase "if possible," which implies sometimes it is *not* possible.

Unless two people in a relationship are willing to come together humbly and do the work, sometimes we have to learn to move on when a relationship doesn't.

My heart is sensitive to people who want relationships to work with all their hearts. I want to encourage you with some truths straight from my journal that I think will really help you today no matter how this is currently playing out in your life:

1. Redemption with God is possible even when reconciliation is not.

One of the hardest but most encouraging lessons that I've learned is that God can still make our stories beautiful even if the story doesn't end the way we thought it would. We have to be careful not to confuse redemption with reunion. Reunion or reconciliation requires two people who are willing to come back together and do the hard work. Redemption, though, is between you and God. God can redeem your life even if damaged human relationships don't come back together. And you and I can forgive even if the relationship never gets restored.

It's incredibly freeing to forgive and not have to wait on the other person who may or may not ever be willing or want to talk this through. Forgiveness isn't always about doing something for a human relationship but rather about being obedient to what God has instructed us to do.

2. You can only be held accountable for what you say and do.

When put in a hard situation where our hearts are completely broken, we often find ourselves doing and saying things that betray who we really are. But some of the best advice that

I've given to some of my friends is this: *prove them wrong*. I'm not saying it to make a statement about the other person. It's to make a statement of dignity about you. Reclaiming your dignity and redeeming your integrity is your choice from here on out.

3. You don't have to know why they hurt you to get better.

You don't have to know why they misunderstood you, betrayed you, didn't love you and protect you or stay like they should have stayed. Their reasons are multilayered with a mysterious mix of their own pain, heartbreak, or soul wrestling. And in the end, they may not even know all the reasons that they made the choices they did.

Here's something I wrote in my journal that gave me permission to move on when I never really knew why everything happened:

Knowing why is no gift at all if it never makes sense. Maybe they love themselves too much or much too little. Maybe their heart was too disconnected or hard or brittle. Soft hearts don't break or beat or belittle. But broken hearts with unhealed pasts can often be found traveling wrong paths. They hurt, they sting, they say words they really don't mean. The pain they project is just an effort to protect all that feels so incredibly fragile inside of them.

Friend, if you want to move on, if you want to heal and lay down what hurts, it's 100 percent your choice to make. The steps needed are yours to take. You can move on from here. In a good way. In a healthy way. Healing is yours for the taking and yours for the keeping.

A statement to remember as I walk into today:

You don't have to know why they hurt you to get better.

EVENING

I find it so interesting that the original phrase for goodbye in the late 1500s was "God Be with Ye." The contraction of that phrase was "Godbwye," which eventually became "goodbye." I've sat with the thought of goodbyes being more of a sending off with God rather than a slammed door, a contact deleted, and a remaining puddle of angst. Even if the relationship can't move forward, I would like a little more "God be with you" in my goodbyes.

Let's try this with some of the relationships in our lives. Sometimes it feels awkward and awful. Sometimes we're in so much pain, it's hard to muster up any energy to do anything but grit our teeth and blast it all out with our counselors. But what if the thought of "God be with you" is really what our hearts need as we face our heartbreaking goodbyes? Even if you can't say it to that person, you can pray it in your heart.

Before we go to bed tonight, I want to invite you to try something. The other night I closed my eyes and pictured Jesus' hands. I mentally started placing all the memories one by one into His strong, carpentry-calloused, nail-pierced, grace-gripped hands. I asked the Lord to help me whisper "God be with you" over each memory. I asked Jesus to help me release some of the memories, hold on to others, and make peace with all that I could. You can do this too.

This exercise of surrender hasn't settled everything yet. But it was a start. And I believe that through this hard but holy process, Jesus is working to heal both your heart and mine.

Lord, let it be so.

SOMETHING TO RELEASE BACK TO GOD FROM TODAY:

_____

_____

A PRAYER TO RECEIVE BEFORE TOMORROW:

God, be with me in every goodbye that I face. Whether it is for a season or forever, I trust that on the other side of this goodbye is something good. When a goodbye is necessary, I will look to You to hold me close and guide me through to what the next season of my life will hold. Help me release some of the memories, hold on to others, and make peace with all I can. I know I cannot do any of this on my own, but with Your help, healing is possible. In Jesus' name, amen.

DAY

50

You're Going
to Make It

Being confident of this, that he who began
a good work in you will carry it on to
completion until the day of Christ Jesus.

PHILIPPIANS 1:6

MORNING

As we reach our final day together in these pages, I just want to say I'm so proud of you, sweet friend.

I'm proud of you for showing up here. With your pain, your confusion, your unanswered questions and prayers, your desire to heal. I'm overwhelmed with gratitude that you would allow me to be your friend as we've walked through this book together, as you also journey through your own life circumstances.

To wrap up our time, I want us to have a marked moment together that we won't let each other stop here. We won't let each other quit. We will keep encouraging each other onward and upward in healing and growth and forgiveness and beauty. As I've said before, the longer I live, the more I see healing less as a destination and more as a daily choice. We're all on a journey. So let's keep making the daily choice to pursue growth and healing together: "Being confident of this, that he who began a good work in you will carry it on to completion until the day of Christ Jesus" (Philippians 1:6).

Growth and healing will look different through different seasons we experience. Sometimes growth will look like

Believing there's more ahead in life and new joys we don't want to miss.
Moving forward with peace and healthier perspectives.
Saying yes to the doors God opens for us and the assignments He has for us.
Accomplishing exciting and important things.
Pursuing healing with trusted, safe voices in our inner circle.
Easing the loneliness ache in others (and then seeing it beautifully eased in us).
Trusting God with it all while declaring with even more confidence that He is good.

Keep pursuing growth toward good and godly pursuits. And remember, don't get discouraged by the inevitable setbacks you may encounter after you close this book—growth and healing require dings. This journey may require a cracking and breaking and a breaking away from what was to form a healthier "new."

As we develop, growth may require us to face some messy situations. As we reach for the new, growth may require us to address old, unhealthy patterns or attitudes. Just as a seed must experience cracking and breaking so new growth can come forth, our growth requires the same.

Growth and healing come as a package deal with some hardships that won't make sense. I suspect I'm not telling you something you don't already know. But here's something that maybe you haven't thought through: Yes, growth may require dings and cracks and breaks. But growth doesn't require accusation.

That voice that tries to assign debilitating labels to you sees your potential for growth as a threat. The voice of the accuser belongs to Satan. Your growth and healing are part of your testimony. And you know what Satan doesn't want you to know today?

This verse: "For the accuser of our brothers and sisters has been thrown down, the one who accuses them before our God day and night. And they overcame him because of the blood of the Lamb and because of the word of their testimony" (Revelation 12:10–11 NASB).

Satan doesn't want you to know how powerful your testimony is. He doesn't want you to know that your expressions of God-honoring, Jesus-empowering truths subdue and overcome him and his accusations. He wants to derail and discourage you in your healing progress so that you never allow what you've been through to turn into a testimony for others to hear.

Because testimonies are powerful tools against him.

This journey might be full of questions and tears and a quiet pulling back to gather yourself. But from growth come powerful testimonies.

Don't forget this, friend. You're going to make it. You're going to be okay. More than okay. You're going to continue to grow, heal, and flourish into a strong and stable woman walking in victory. I pray the devil regrets ever messing with you . . . and me!

And in case you forget, I'll always be here in these pages to encourage you.

Onward and upward, my dear sisters.

Onward and upward, indeed.

A statement to remember as I walk into today:

Testimonies are powerful tools against the Enemy.

You know what's hard about being hurt and deciding to heal? Life goes on. You know what's good about being hurt and deciding to heal? Life goes on.

Because that's what life has a habit of doing.

The world has not stopped spinning.

And your world has not shrunk down to this hard reality being the sum total of you. You're made for more than this difficult relationship or experience defining you. There is so much more to discover and uncover.

You need to remember how big the world is again. And how capable our God is who created this world.

There are still wonderful people to meet. There are still deserving people to help. There are still honest souls both young and old. Make a bucket list. Make a cancel list. Make a "let's just dance it all out" song list.

Step outside and look up at the sky. It's not falling. Maybe your world isn't falling apart.

Maybe you are falling back together.

Recently, I wrote a poem in my journal. I needed some closure that I knew I may never get from the one who hurt me. (Side note: I drove my mom nuts when I was a little girl by constantly writing poems and country songs. I would stand on the fireplace hearth and beg her to be my audience as I recited my poems written on parchment paper with burnt edges. Why did I always burn the edges? Who knows? Anyhow . . .)

Here's what I wrote:

> I fell.
> I fell in love.
> I fell into your arms.
> I fell hard.
> I fell for who I thought you were.
> I fell for believing we were meant to be.
> I fell for overriding my discernment.
> I fell for the lies.
> I fell apart.
> I fell for the false hope.
> I fell apart again.
> I fell hard.

I fell back into place.

I fell together.

And then I stopped falling and started rising.

We all have to make the decision either to live a lie or live fully alive. Rest tonight, beautiful friend. For tomorrow, it is time to rise.

Together. Amen.

SOMETHING TO RELEASE BACK TO GOD FROM TODAY:

_____

_____

A PRAYER TO RECEIVE BEFORE TOMORROW:

Lord, thank You for all the ways You're moving in my life. Thank You for helping me process, reflect, move forward, and heal. No matter what I'm processing from the past or what comes my way in the future, thank You for being my guide and strength. I know I'm going to make it through anything because I have You. Help me continue to be a source of encouragement to others walking through their own healing journeys as well. In Jesus' name, amen.

Places You Can Turn to When You Need Help

Dear friend,

I hope this devotional book has provided encouragement for you in whatever you're facing right now. For some, though, you may find this is only a starting point for healing. I am not a licensed counselor and this book doesn't take the place of therapy, but please be comforted in knowing there are many therapists who are ready and willing to help navigate anything you need help processing. I have benefited from the help of a licensed Christian counselor, and I am so thankful for their guidance. If you need to find a professional Christian counselor in your area, the American Association of Christian Counselors has recommendations listed on their website at aacc.net. Your church may also have a list of trusted Christian counselors they recommend.

I would also love to invite you to tune into the *Therapy & Theology* podcast. During these episodes, I team up with my personal counselor Jim Cress and Proverbs 31 Ministries Director of Theology and Research, Dr. Joel Muddamalle, to help you work through what you're walking through. Together, we'll talk about the real issues you're experiencing in your life and relationships and help you move forward. You can find all of these episodes at therapyandtheologypodcast.com.

I'm praying for you, friend.

Much love,

About the Author

Photo credit: Meshali Mitchell

LYSA TERKEURST is president of Proverbs 31 Ministries and the author of more than twenty-five books, including *It's Not Supposed to Be This Way* and the #1 *New York Times* bestsellers *Forgiving What You Can't Forget* and *Uninvited*. But to those who know her best, she's just a simple girl with a well-worn Bible who proclaims hope in the midst of good times and heartbreaking realities.

Lysa lives with her family in Charlotte, North Carolina. Connect with her on a daily basis, see what she's working on next, and follow her speaking schedule:

Website: www.LysaTerKeurst.com
(Click on "events" to inquire about
having Lysa speak at your event.)
www.Proverbs31.org
Facebook: www.Facebook.com/OfficialLysa
Instagram: @LysaTerKeurst
Twitter: @LysaTerKeurst

Notes

Day 2: Living with the Mystery

1. Karen Plum, "Unlocking Psychological Safety," Advanced Workplace Associates, July 6, 2020, https://www.advanced-workplace.com/unlocking-psychological-safety/.

Day 40: I Don't Like Being Caught Off Guard

1. Oxford University Press, Lexico, s.v. "steady," July 14, 2021, http://www.lexico.com/definition/steady.

2. Oxford University Press., Lexico, s.v. "unsteady," July 14, 2021, http://www.lexico.com/definition/unsteady.

Day 44: Consider the Source

1. Dictionary.com, based on the *Random House Unabridged Dictionary* (New York: Random House, 2022), s.v. "folly," http://www.dictionary.com/browse/folly.

2. "How the Brain Takes Criticism," CBS News, March 2, 2014, http://www.cbsnews.com/news/how-the-brain-takes-criticism.

Day 45: Encouragement for a Grieving Heart

1. Rodrigues, A. M. (2014). *Atonement*. D. Mangum, D. R. Brown, R. Klippenstein, & R. Hurst (Eds.), *Lexham Theological Wordbook*. Bellingham, WA: Lexham Press.

2. Donald Guthrie, *Hebrews, Tyndale New Testament Commentaries* (Downers Grove, IL: InterVarsity Press, 2015), 96.

3. J. H. Merle D'Aubigné, *History of the Great Reformation of the Sixteenth Century in Germany, Switzerland*, trans. H. White, vol. 4 (New York: Robert Carter, 1846), 183.

Day 48: The Power to Live Out Scripture Even When It Feels Impossible

1. Walter Grundmann, "Δύναμαι, Δυνατός, Δυνατέω, Ἀδύνατος, Ἀδυνατέω, Δύναμις, Δυνάστης, Δυναμόω, Ἐνδυναμόω," ed. Gerhard Kittel, Geoffrey W. Bromiley, and Gerhard Friedrich, *Theological Dictionary of the New Testament* (Grand Rapids, MI: Eerdmans, 1964–), 284.

What Should I Read From Lysa Next?

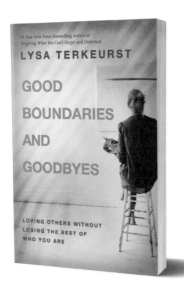
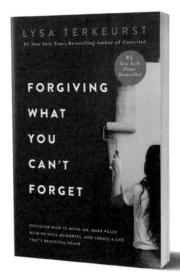

Good Boundaries and Goodbyes:
Loving Others Without Losing
the Best of Who You Are

Forgiving What You Can't Forget:
Discover How to Move On,
Make Peace with Painful
Memories, and Create a Life
That's Beautiful Again

What if our time with God has *little* to do
with quieting *everything* **around us**, and
instead has *everything* to do with making an
appointment to *quiet* things **within us**?

Stop feeling overwhelmed in your quiet
time struggles today by **downloading the free
First 5 mobile app** at
http://www.first5.org.